CHESTER
MEMORIES

The publishers would like to thank the following companies for their support in the production of this book

Main Sponsor
Corus

Arts & Crafts Studio

Crabwall Hall Residential Home

Chester Market

Cochranes of Chester

Dutton & Hallmark

The King's School

Maltby's of Chester

The Queen's School

University of Chester

Urenco

First published in Great Britain by True North Books Limited
England HX3 6AE
01422 344344

ISBN 1 903204 83 6

Text, design and origination by True North Books Limited
Printed and bound by The Amadeus Press Limited

CHESTER MEMORIES

Contents

Introduction

Welcome to 'Chester Memories'. This book is the latest in a series that revisits the city that our parents and grandparents knew so well. Older readers will recall many of the forgotten scenes for themselves. Younger ones will be able to put in place the sights and sounds of 20th century Chester that they were told about with such affection. Unlike many others, the face of our city architecture has not altered dramatically, but the pace and style of life has changed from the days in which our grandparents held sway. How often have we wished that we could have spoken at more depth with them about the world they knew? Although we may have missed that opportunity, there is still the chance to gain some insight into an era when coinage was in the 'lsd' that referred to pounds, shillings and pence and not some form of hallucinatory drug or when going on a trip meant a day out in Colwyn Bay and not out of your skull!

All the photographs within have been enhanced by the attachment of captions intended to inform, or even provoke comment. They are not image titles but text designed to highlight elements of each photograph and, on occasion, offer a pithy outlook on the background or times in which the scenes were observed. Hopefully, this will prompt the reader into making his or her own interpretation. Feel free to disagree, for then we have succeeded in stimulating discussion. That can only be of benefit as we think back over how life might have been in the times depicted, or how it really was if we are old enough to recall those days. Perhaps for some of us those memories have a hazy hue and the photographs will help bring everything flooding back. The camera never lies, though its angles might offer a slightly different perspective.

This collection of delightful photographs brings back to life a time when attitudes and society in general were so different. There really was an age when mobile phones did not disturb the peace of the lounge bar in the pub. Men offered their seats to women on the bus, or touched their hats in the streets when wishing a lady a good morning. Children called

their teachers 'Sir' and 'Miss' and never realised that the adults lecturing them had an existence outside the schoolroom. Supermarkets and shopping malls, ugly concrete office blocks and super fast highways and ring roads were still to come when many of these images were captured. The book makes no apology for indulging in that warm glow of reflecting on the past. Times have changed, not always for the better, however not everything new is to be dismissed as a lowering of standards. 'Chester Memories' will also remind the reader of wartime days, when we feared the worst as bombers flew overhead on missions to Liverpool, but it is with the aggressive intentions of other invaders than the Nazis that the real history of the city begins.

It was in 79 AD that the Romans established a camp on a small sandstone ridge at the head of the estuary of the river Dee. The location was selected as the headquarters of the 20th Legion and named Deva or Castra Devana. It was an ideal spot as it provided access to a deep harbour and commanded one of the main crossing points of the Dee. Deva was a base for the Roman fleet and soon was established as a major military settlement, augmented by large numbers of civilians who were attracted to the town by the opportunity to trade with the Romans or provide support services. Of course, the Romans had more to offer than their fighting skills. They laid streets, provided underfloor heating in a number of houses and built a 7,000 seat amphitheatre. They came to set up a fortress from which they could control the local population, but left behind a culture that still fascinates historians and archaeologists today. Some readers of this book may well have ancestors who date back to the Valeria Victrix Legion as many soldiers married local girls and had Roman-British families. Eventually, as the power of Rome declined, the invading forces were withdrawn. By the start of the 5th century, most of the forts and towns that they developed were abandoned. They left behind a legacy of roads and place names that remain with us, not to mention the innumerable coins, pots, tiles, inscribed tablets etc that have been unearthed in digs over the years. Of course, in Chester's case, we have the obvious evidence of the city walls from which the modern visitor can gaze inwards to view the city as it has developed over 2,000 years. Alternatively, he can look out across the Dee and imagine being stationed under a standard

adorned with an eagle as, with gladius in hand, he was part of a mighty, all-conquering force that was master of all he surveyed.

Once the Romans had gone, Deva sank into comparative obscurity. There were the occasional raids up the Dee by Norsemen from across the North Sea with the customary pillaging and whatever else it was that Vikings did. However, these were quiet years, but gradually the Saxons came to call and began to re-establish such towns and remodel them for their own purposes. In 875 the relics of Saint Werburgh, a Saxon saint and daughter of a Mercian king, were brought here for safekeeping and a religious community founded in her honour. This became one of the country's foremost monastic establishments, flourishing until dissolution in the 16th century. By the early 10th century, this town was a bustling and vibrant Mercian settlement, trading with north Wales. Aetheflaeda, the daughter of Alfred the Great, was the inspiration behind the refortification works. She also commissioned the building of a string of fortresses from Runcorn and eastward towards the Pennine hills. By now, the modern name of Chester was in use and it had regained its glory as a successful and wealthy port.

But, it is to more modern times that we turn in 'Chester Memories'. Somehow, the city has managed to reflect the demands of modern society without compromising its historical identity. The prosperity of the Victorian age provided the wherewithal to shape the face of the modern city. The Rows and the Cathedral were restored, buildings with their distinctive black and white facades were erected and new thoroughfares were cut. But, it is to the sights of the last century that we now turn. Pour yourself a shot of dandelion and burdock, suck on a Spangle and put on a 78 (remember them?) of someone who was popular before even Cliff Richard was heard of. It is the moment to go on that journey back through time. Dressed in hot pants from the 1970s or cloche hats from the 1920s, return to the days when Biggles ruled the skies and Alf Tupper ran on the track faster than any Olympian. Turning the very first page launches the nostalgia trip. Do not let anything disturb those cherished memories. For some of us Max Bygraves once sang it out clearly with 'Fings ain't what they used to be', so let us now decide if he was right.

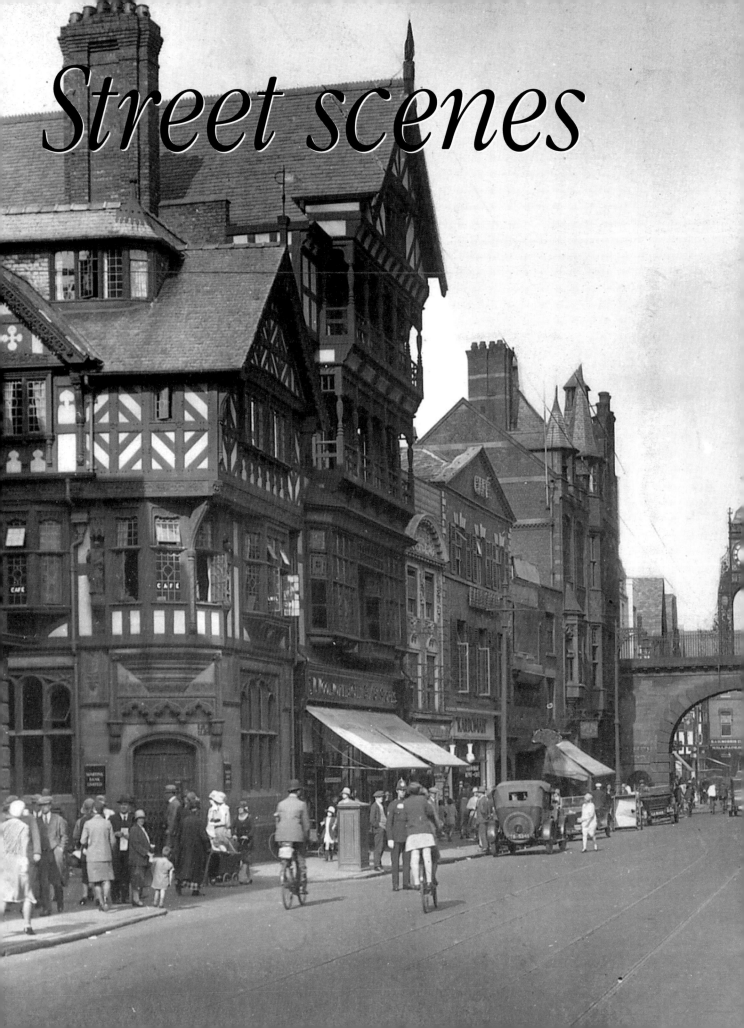

Street scenes

The skirt lengths favoured by fashionable young women in the 1930s were considerably shorter than those worn by their mothers. The older generation had its roots in pre-war Britain when dress hems brushed the floor in the Edwardian era. The modern miss had come through the years when they gained suffrage and this new freedom was reflected in the more carefree way in which they dressed and behaved. Sadly, for many, this decade was not the period of growth and prosperity that had been envisaged when Kaiser Bill was finally put in his place. High unemployment and the years of industrial depression meant that the working classes struggled to keep their heads above water. This was not evident on Eastgate Street, as we look past the 1860 Westminster Bank on the left and along to the clock at Eastgate, because those out and about appear to be the more middle class of shoppers, to tell from their clothing. Lower classes would not have been able to afford to shop in the more exclusive outlets in the city. They were skimping along, though at least they were no longer living in the insanitary slums of the courts that used to be on Foregate Street. Many had been rehoused in Newton, Blacon and Lache where they could at least be healthy if not wealthy.

Eastgate, as seen c1935, was obviously busy and the horse and cart being led away from the clock tower was on its way out of usefulness as well. Motorcars and lorries had come to stay as a different sort of horsepower arrived to dominate the scene. The men near the bicycle on the left surveyed the passing from one era to another, but did so from separate perspectives. The trio on the pavement was marked as working class. Flat caps were the giveaway, for they were the uniform of those who got their hands dirty for a living. Standing just away from them, as probably befitted one with a managerial position, the chap under the homburg did not mix too well with those who were his social inferiors. He had little regard for those from the humbler reaches of society. Not everything changes quickly. Remember the comedy sketch in television's 'Frost Report' in the 1960s when John Cleese, Ronnie Barker and Ronnie Corbett looked variously up and down at each other? The scene could have been acted out on Eastgate nearly half a century earlier. The half timbered buildings on the right were occupied by WH Smith's booksellers and Stewart King's tailoring shop. Next to this latter outlet, the distinctive shape of the Burton building would see trade blossom as the 'tailor of taste' made his mark on the city.

Below: This view along to the cathedral shows St Werburgh Street as it appeared in the 1930s. The two men in earnest conversation outside Parrs Bank, designed by George Williams and later the National Westminster, with the offices of the Norwich Union above their heads, were facing the Bank of Liverpool. This latter building eventually became Martin's Bank before being taken over by Barclays in the 1960s. The Tamil Café and Rubber Shop further along on the right were housed in the buildings that John Douglas designed in the late 1890s. St Werburgh Street and the cathedral were named for the member of Mercian royalty whose bones found a resting place here in 875. She died in the early years of the 8th century and the minster founded on this site became a popular shrine for pilgrims in the Middle Ages. The saint's remains had been brought from Hanbury to ensure safekeeping from the ravages of the Danish hordes who regularly raided this part of Britain. Modern visitors to the cathedral run the gamut of pavement preachers who often congregate in this vicinity, urging the faithless to repent and offering free leaflets and papers containing text from the Bible. Unfortunately for them, most of those passing by seem more interested in the text messages from their mobile phones.

Right: Even in the 1920s, Eastgate Street was a busy thoroughfare. Two women in the foreground seem to be chancing their arms as they cross from St Peter's Church towards Bridge Street. Such was the growing popularity of the motorcar that a traffic policeman had to be employed at the junction with Northgate. Suitably attired in a white coat, his was the awesome task of keeping everything moving through streets that had never been intended to cater for a high volume of modern transport. This would be an ever increasing problem that would eventually lead to notorious logjams of traffic with the inevitable demand for ring roads and pedestrianised areas in the later years of the 20th century. The bobby on point duty at The Cross had taken up station outside The Etonian. This was a tailor for gentlemen, as befitting the shop's name. Made to measure suits for the well to do were crafted with as much care and expertise as shown by any artist or sculptor working upon a fine creation. Gentlemen did not purchase their clothing in a supermarket 80 years ago. The Etonian traded on the opposite corner from St Peter's and is now Raffles, an oriental restaurant. This church possibly had a Saxon foundation in the time of Aetheflaeda, King Alfred's daughter, and its interior dates back some 500 years, though it was largely restored in 1887.

Although this photograph is not dated, must date back to the early years of the last century from the evidence of the ground length skirt of the woman on the right. This would be at a time before television had even been thought of and national radio as an entertainment media was still just a pipe dream. The occasional primitive cinema, showing slides or a very short reel of film, was still more likely to be a theatre or music hall than a purpose built edifice. Live entertainment, with actors, comedians, speciality acts and singers, were what pulled in the crowds a hundred years ago. One of the biggest treats for locals was the week that the circus came to town. They turned out in droves to line the streets as the parade passed by. For the circus proprietors this was a good way in which to advertise the forthcoming attractions. A marching band led the way, followed by camels, dancing dogs, prancing ponies and lumbering elephants. Clowns with large feet and gaily decorated faces sprayed water onto squealing children and everyone oohed and aahed as the acrobats tumbled their way down the street. Men on stilts handed out leaflets, fire-eaters behaved like dragons and pretty trapeze artists and tightrope walkers flashed their eyes and other parts of their anatomies at ogling menfolk. When the show under the big top eventually got under way, it was everything the public had expected and the performers were treated to long bursts of tumultuous applause.

Below: By the late 1950s Britain was entering a period of high optimism. The dark, dank days of gloom and doom that permeated the austerity of the immediate postwar era were disappearing. Just to make sure that we realised it, Prime Minister Harold Macmillan announced that 'We have never had it so good'. These were the days when washing machines, vacuum cleaners, fridges and televisions became the sort of possessions that were within the financial reach of every household. Employment was high and wages provided for more than just basic necessities. There was money left over for luxuries, too. Families might not be able to splash out the full amount for everything, but there was the wonder of hire purchase and the tills in the electrical goods shops rang merrily. On Bridge Street the Rows did good business. Family saloons, now not just affordable by the middle classes, brought shoppers into the city. The Morris Minor, Ford Popular and Standard 8 bowled along the streets and parked outside the establishments where their passengers wanted to shop. Imagine that luxury today as you struggle from a Pay and Display spot through the pouring rain. The layout of the Rows, one of the features of Chester's originality, dates back to the 13th century when the first covered galleries above street level where designed. They are just one of the things about Chester that sets it apart from other cities.

Above: Afternoon tea was being taken in the Rows on Bridge Street, probably in the 1920s if the parade of limousines is anything to go by. For a moment one can be forgiven for thinking that Al Capone or Babyface Nelson might leap on the running board of one of the cars and spray everyone with machine gun fire. But this is Chester, not Chicago, and Cestrians have always been such genteel folk. Men in boaters and striped blazers, cigarettes idly dangling from their fingers, chit-chatted about the state of the economy and the nonsense caused by 'those dreadful mining chaps' who were threatening to withdraw their labour because their employers threatened to cut their wages or extend their working week. 'They should thank their lucky stars they have a job after all, don't you know'. Ladies demurely stirred their tea and lifted their cups, little finger poised ever so daintily, towards rosebud lips as they discussed the cloche hats and flapper skirts that the young girls favoured. They spoke guardedly about what the Pankhursts had achieved, now that the over 30s could vote. They had heard that all women over the age of 21 would be able to access the ballot box by the end of the decade. Soon it was time to order another drop scone and wonder, 'Is there honey still for tea?'

Above: Work on the inner ring road was not commenced until 1960, even though suggestions for one had been mooted as far back as 1945. Until the plans were put into practice, traffic ploughed through the city centre in ever increasing numbers. Foregate Street was just one of those having to cope with the choking up of the traffic and the choking up of our lungs as we took in those noxious fumes. Seen here, with WH Smith and MacFisheries to the left, cars and lorries streaming towards the camera are grinding to a halt. This was a common sight in 1956 as traffic from north Wales, connecting with Lancashire and north Cheshire, had to work its way over Grosvenor Bridge and through The Cross. The motorcar was becoming a boon to ordinary families as new models rolling off the Austin and Morris assembly lines came into the showrooms at affordable prices. Postwar rationing was a thing of the past, albeit only by a few years, and Britons looked forward optimistically to better times ahead. What could symbolise that better than the ownership of a shiny, new car? Unfortunately, it took ages to get anywhere. Day trippers to Rhyl or Llandudno fretted in advance about the crawl through Chester. It was even worse along the coast at Queensferry, where families have been known to picnic at the roadside, despairing of ever reaching the beach they had set out for hours earlier.

Below: It is another busy day on Bridge Street, the pavements crowded with shoppers. Traffic moves along in both directions and we can see parked vehicles by the roadside. What a luxury this is to our eyes, some 45 years or so from the date of this photograph. These would be a sight to delight the heart of a modern traffic warden who would instantly bear down on the cars and vans, pencil and ticket in hand. Bridge Street is now pedestrianised along its northern half, separated off by bollards and telephone boxes. The buses seen here are heading towards St Michael's Church, on the corner with Pepper Street where Lower Bridge Street begins. These vehicles have come from the vicinity of St Peter's Church, seen in the distance, that was restored in the late 1880s at about the same time as a number of buildings, some designed by TM Lockwood, first graced the area around The Cross. This picture proves that not only have times and motoring styles changed, but so have some moral attitudes. The hawk-eyed reader should be able to spot the bicycle propped up at the kerb, just below the antiques shop. We did once live in an age when people respected one another's property. It would not last five minutes today, unless it was padlocked and chained to an immovable object. Even then, some villain would probably steal the immovable object; 'only having a laugh, mate'.

Left: Chester has a series of gates that guard the entrances to the city. The clock at Eastgate, after Big Ben perhaps one of Britain's most photographed timepieces, makes this part of the city walls the most noticeable. Eastgate marks the point where Foregate Street meets Eastgate Street and, at any time of day, people can be seen standing on the walls under the clock, looking down on the mass of humanity below. The walls around Chester are a permanent reminder of the days when the Romans arrived to establish their fortress at Deva in AD 79. However, the stoneworks are not the original edifices as the invaders first built wooden palisades, towers and gateways. In about AD 100 stone walls were added to the front of the earth ramparts and the towers and gateways rebuilt. These survived long after the Romans had gone home, several centuries later. Although the Saxons refortified Chester, it was the Normans who completed the circuit of the walls, adding new features as they did. It was in the 18th century when fashion dictated that the gentry should promenade the walls and it was a common sight to see young couples strolling the two mile circuit, carefully shadowed by chaperones. The wall is now a scheduled ancient monument and is cared for by the city council.

Above: At one time, every town and city had its own department store, one established by locals that knew the inhabitants' tastes and understood their needs. For many years, these stores resisted the 20th century competition brought against them by such giants as John Lewis, Marks and Spencer and Littlewoods. Sadly, one by one most were picked off. Paulden's in Manchester is no more, Jenner in Edinburgh has disappeared and Harvey's of Guildford was swallowed up by the House of Fraser. Somehow, Brown's on Eastgate Street has managed to survive and combat the moguls with a mixture of success and endurance. Seen here on the left, where people are alighting from the bus, it owes its existence to the founder, Susannah Brown, back in the late 1700s. Boasting five floors of 'fashion and furnishing', the store has been a byword for quality and charm ever since its doors first opened. It is not just adults who enjoyed their time shopping, browsing or taking tea, as children were always fascinated by the tubes containing money and paperwork. They whizzed across the store, driven by compressed air, from the counters to the cashiers and back again. Of course, Christmas time was special for the little ones as a visit to Santa's grotto was a must. It is now part of Debenhams. But has retained its name and sense of history. The policeman in the roadway probably did not get his gloves from Brown's as they would be standard issue and not the height of fashion for directing traffic!

Much of Eastgate Street is now part of the pedestrianised shopping centre of the city and this photograph dates from the time when traffic traversed the centre without recourse to the ring road that was built to funnel vehicles away from and around Chester. Many of the shops along here now have new ground floor facades, but most of them have retained the sense of architectural history in their upper floors. The view along the street at that first floor and above perspective is similar to that seen in this image of half a century ago. The Grosvenor Shopping Precinct now abuts the south side of Eastgate Street without intruding on its air of elegance. It takes its name from the family name of the Earls of Westminster who were landowners and benefactors, particularly in the 19th century. The building of Grosvenor Bridge in 1827 was aided by a £1,000 donation from the then Earl. On Eastgate Street, the prestigious Grosvenor Hotel opened its doors to its first paying guests in 1866 on the site of the former Royal Hotel. Designed by TM Penson, the hotel was originally owned by Richard, the 2nd Marquess of Westminster. It has long been the place in Chester to stay if you are of certain means or wish for a short course in being pampered.

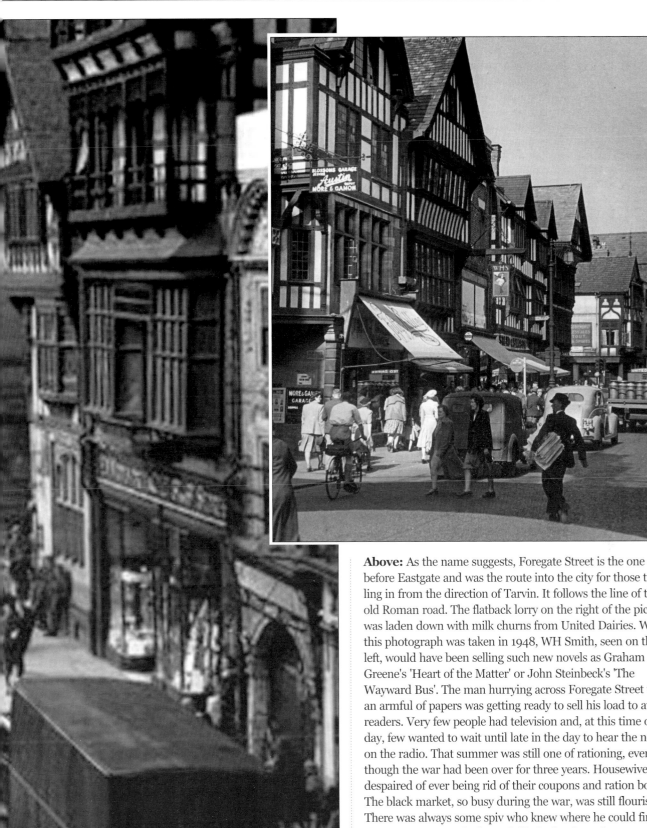

Above: As the name suggests, Foregate Street is the one before Eastgate and was the route into the city for those travelling in from the direction of Tarvin. It follows the line of the old Roman road. The flatback lorry on the right of the picture was laden down with milk churns from United Dairies. When this photograph was taken in 1948, WH Smith, seen on the left, would have been selling such new novels as Graham Greene's 'Heart of the Matter' or John Steinbeck's 'The Wayward Bus'. The man hurrying across Foregate Street with an armful of papers was getting ready to sell his load to avid readers. Very few people had television and, at this time of the day, few wanted to wait until late in the day to hear the news on the radio. That summer was still one of rationing, even though the war had been over for three years. Housewives despaired of ever being rid of their coupons and ration books. The black market, so busy during the war, was still flourishing. There was always some spiv who knew where he could find that extra item not freely available in the shops, but at a price, of course. On a lighter note, Freddie Mills boxed his way to the light heavyweight championship of the world for us and, at last, Australia's star cricketer Don Bradman bowed out, albeit with a duck thanks to the surprised bowler, Eric Hollies.

Above: The policewoman on point duty looks to have her hands full trying to keep the streets of Chester from becoming snarled up. It was ever thus as the car owning population increased dramatically in the late 1950s and early 1960s. What had been a luxury item for the middle classes eventually became every family's run of the mill acquisition. The toll on our roads and the environment became worrying as carriageways crumbled or were of insufficient width to cope with the volume and exhaust fumes pumped their noxious gases into the air around us. Motoring became part of our daily life as we abandoned buses to get to work and the railways to reach our holiday destination. The light coloured Morris Traveller, with its distinctive wooden framed coachwork, sported a GB sticker. The occupants were obviously part of the pioneering holiday movement in Britain that had turned to the Continent for its vacations. Package holidays in Spain that involved air travel were becoming more attractive by the minute as affluent Britons had more cash in their pockets than ever before. Others, like those in the Traveller, drove down to the south coast and its ferry terminals, crossing to Calais. Le Havre and St Malo before heading off to a Breton holiday under canvas. This photograph was taken on 29 July 1966 and marked the official reopening of Eastgate Street after refurbishment and redecoration. The following day England would beat West Germany 4-2 in soccer's World Cup Final at Wembley.

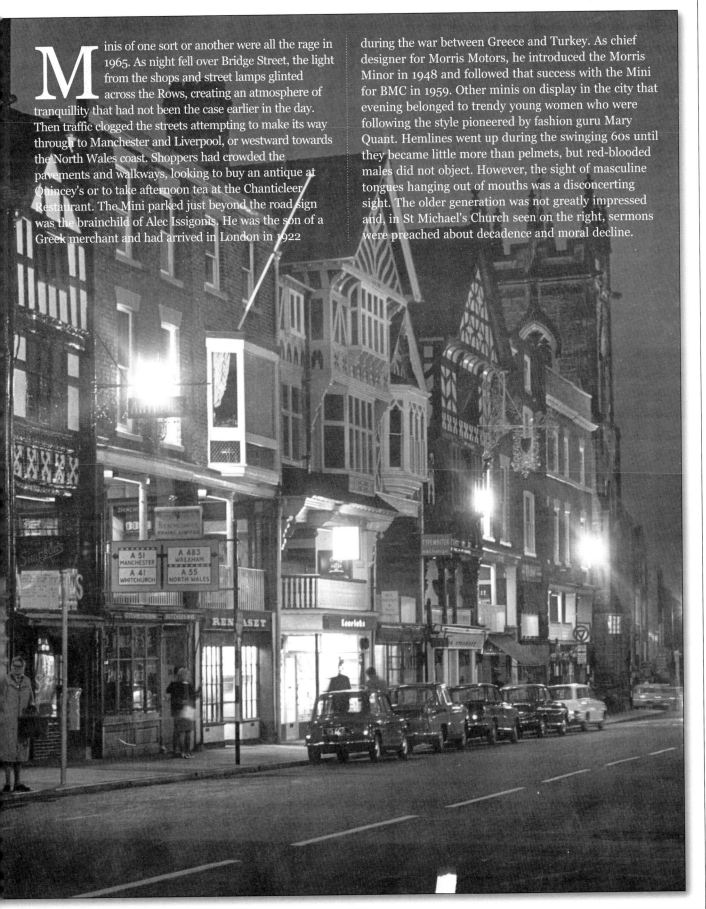

Minis of one sort or another were all the rage in 1965. As night fell over Bridge Street, the light from the shops and street lamps glinted across the Rows, creating an atmosphere of tranquillity that had not been the case earlier in the day. Then traffic clogged the streets attempting to make its way through to Manchester and Liverpool, or westward towards the North Wales coast. Shoppers had crowded the pavements and walkways, looking to buy an antique at Quincey's or to take afternoon tea at the Chanticleer Restaurant. The Mini parked just beyond the road sign was the brainchild of Alec Issigonis. He was the son of a Greek merchant and had arrived in London in 1922 during the war between Greece and Turkey. As chief designer for Morris Motors, he introduced the Morris Minor in 1948 and followed that success with the Mini for BMC in 1959. Other minis on display in the city that evening belonged to trendy young women who were following the style pioneered by fashion guru Mary Quant. Hemlines went up during the swinging 60s until they became little more than pelmets, but red-blooded males did not object. However, the sight of masculine tongues hanging out of mouths was a disconcerting sight. The older generation was not greatly impressed and, in St Michael's Church seen on the right, sermons were preached about decadence and moral decline.

At leisure

It is to be hoped that Raymond and Bernard Davies have someone a little bit older than them in the other end of this vessel as they contemplate a day's boating on the river in 1922. Let us pray that daddy returned from the front four years earlier to regain his place in the family household and that he was the one sitting in the bows or taking the picture. The boys look to be well prepared for a day out. The whopping wicker hamper surely had plenty of tuck, for this pair of youngsters look to be well nourished and capable of scoffing their fair share. Interestingly, the younger boy is operating a gramophone. Obviously, he was a technological whiz kid in the making. The machine, more correctly called a phonograph as 'gramophone' was a brand name, used a disposable needle, held in place by a small screw, at the end of a manually operated, curved stylus arm. It was the sort of equipment that was a mainly middle class possession, being comparatively expensive to purchase. The record on the turntable might well have reflected the status of the owner in that it was a pressing of an operatic piece by Gigli or Caruso. A family with more modern tastes would have opted for 'I wish I could shimmy like my sister Kate'.

Below: The years following World War I were a mixed bag. Prime Minister David Lloyd George promised the nation that the government would create a land fit for heroes. That was largely a pious pipedream as men who had given their all in the trenches returned to a country whose economy was in tatters. Investment in industry and Britain's infrastructure had been put on hold as all monies and concentration were focused on the war effort. The country was down at heel and cash in short supply. The first to suffer were the lower classes, many living in substandard houses and working for a pittance. Working class women were disgruntled, many having to leave jobs that they had held for several years while their menfolk fought at the front. Yet, for ladies of more comfortable means, the 1920s were a revolution in freedom, opportunity and acceptance. The flapper era, the time of the emancipated young woman, began after the war with the granting of the vote to women over 30, an age limit removed in 1928. The shift of power away from heavy industry and the rise in importance of service industries and office work gave opportunities to those who were a cut above factory work. Women had a new independence and it showed in their fashions and attitudes as well. Here a bevy of beauty on the Dee, showing a leg that scandalised dad, had no need of men to row them. They could mange quite well on their own.

Above: Jolly good boating weather is not a phrase to be applied to this scene showing a frozen River Dee. It would be more appropriate to hum 'The Skaters' Waltz', that evocative piece of music composed by Strasbourg born Charles Emil Waldteufel, one of the most prolific composers of waltzes and polkas of the 19th century. Whenever his famous tune is played, visions of skates gliding across rinks or frozen wastes immediately come to mind. In these days of global warning and climate change, the opportunity to enjoy open air skating is a rarity for we now have much blander winters than even in our youth, never mind those of our grandparents. As children we always had a snowman in the garden at some point of the year and went whizzing down a hillside on a tin tray. Nowadays, thanks to the way we have treated our planet, those opportunities are becoming rare. There are several instances of the Dee freezing over in the past, but they are all some time ago. The waters solidified in December 1895 and again on 8 February 1917, with a further occurrence recorded on 17 February 1929. Here we can see many people simply enjoying the novelty of promenading on ice, while others stand around chatting or watching the intrepid ones who are attempting to impress with their skating skills. Perhaps some fancied going on and becoming ice champions like Sonja Henie, the Norwegian-born American figure skater who held the world amateur championship for women for ten years and won three Olympic gold medals in the interwar years.

The Queens Park Bridge is an attractive structure spanning the River Dee, or Afon Dyfrdwy if you are of Welsh persuasion. It links Victoria Crescent and the Queens Park district on the south bank with Grosvenor Park and The Groves on the north. The 20 acre parkland, adjacent to the ruined St John's Church, was laid out in 1867 and landscaped by Edward Kemp, a follower of Joseph Paxton, the designer of the Crystal Palace and the great conservatory at Chatsworth. The Groves have provided a peaceful and idyllic spot for picnickers and promenaders for several hundred years and are a vantage point for spectators watching the regular regattas or rowing boats and launches that are a common feature of this stretch of the river. The first bridge across the Dee to be built here, designed by James Dredge, opened in 1852 as a link with what was intended to be the garden suburb of Queens Park, with grand villas and homes designed by Thomas Harrison. However, little materialised and most of the buildings in that vicinity are now of more modern origin. The original bridge was replaced by this suspension structure with a span of 277 feet. It was built by David Rowell and Company and opened in 1923. The cottage to the left still stands today and its successive owners must have counted millions of pairs of feet crossing the bridge in the intervening years.

Below: There were districts within districts half a century ago in that a street or a small area had its own particular identity. Quite often, families lived close by one another, so that gran was just on the next street to us with cousin Flo round the corner. In between were the neighbours, most of whom we regarded as both friends and as part of an extended family. As children we referred to the adults living nearby as 'uncle' and 'auntie'. It was disrespectful to refer to your elders by their Christian names, but using the formal 'Mr' or 'Mrs' seemed too remote. The downside of such proximity was that everybody knew each other's business. No secret was safe for long. On the other hand, there were great advantages. Friends and family so close by meant that, in time of need, there was a shoulder to cry on, a helping hand to be given. This was a time when community spirit was at its height. It would become eroded as the 20th century grew on and people developed a greater mobility in their lifestyles and working patterns. This group of locals were obviously good pals as they seem to be getting together for a day out on the chara. The driver put the packed lunches, buckets and spades and fishing nets in the boot and the happy contingent set off, in all probability, to one of the North Wales resorts such as Llandudno for a day trip that they talked about for weeks.

Above: Blacon, to the west of the city, is one of several districts that owe much of its history to the slum clearance programme of the interwar years. Insanitary, cramped housing was the breeding ground for disease and brevity of life expectancy. Chester, in keeping with most other major towns and cities, tackled the problem by building low cost housing on estates that could be largely self sufficient in that they had their own schools, clinics, pubs, post offices and shops. Recreational areas for youngsters were also deemed to be important as they provided places where children could exercise and let off steam. Every local park had swings, roundabouts, see-saws, rocking horses and slides, but some of the more imaginative ones added some extra features. In Blacon, the kiddies were provided with an adventure play area. With a mixture of tunnels and slopes, the children could act out their fantasies as mountaineers or diamond miners. Alternatively, they could just use the structures for hide and seek or jumping games. A few pretend that they were camping or had built their own dens and brought along bottles of pop and a pack of butties to help them maintain the illusion. In a previous generation, lots of youngsters stayed out for most of the day during school holidays. Parents were quite happy to be told where they were off to and, as long as they were back for tea, content in the knowledge that they were in a secure environment.

Above: The Monkey House at Chester Zoo is claimed to be the largest in Europe. It opened on 7 September 1963 and still continues to attract visitors in their millions today. Anyone in the midlands, northwest of England or north Wales who claims to have visited the zoo is surely a liar, because it really lives up to its name as an attraction. However, not everyone has wholly fond memories. Any teacher telling you that he has enjoyed every school trip he has led here since the start of his career is being economical with the truth. After 30 odd years in the job, the thought of the annual pilgrimage with yet another set of 60 urchins from year three becomes about as attractive as the run up to the production of the Christmas nativity play. A weary soul can only take so much of children being sick on the coach, falling into the penguin pond or giggling stupidly at chimpanzees' bottoms. For most other folk, the occasional visit to Chester Zoo is a joy, particularly so when accompanied by the family for there is so much to do and see in the extensive gardens and paddocks that date back to before the war when GS Mottershead acquired the site. Most families on a visit come well prepared with plenty of food and drink to keep them going, plus a pac-a-mac or two if they have any sense. On a more sombre note, the zoo is often somewhere to spot divorced fathers forlornly trying to entertain their children every second Sunday that they have access. 'Daddy's taking us to the zoo to-morrow' - again.

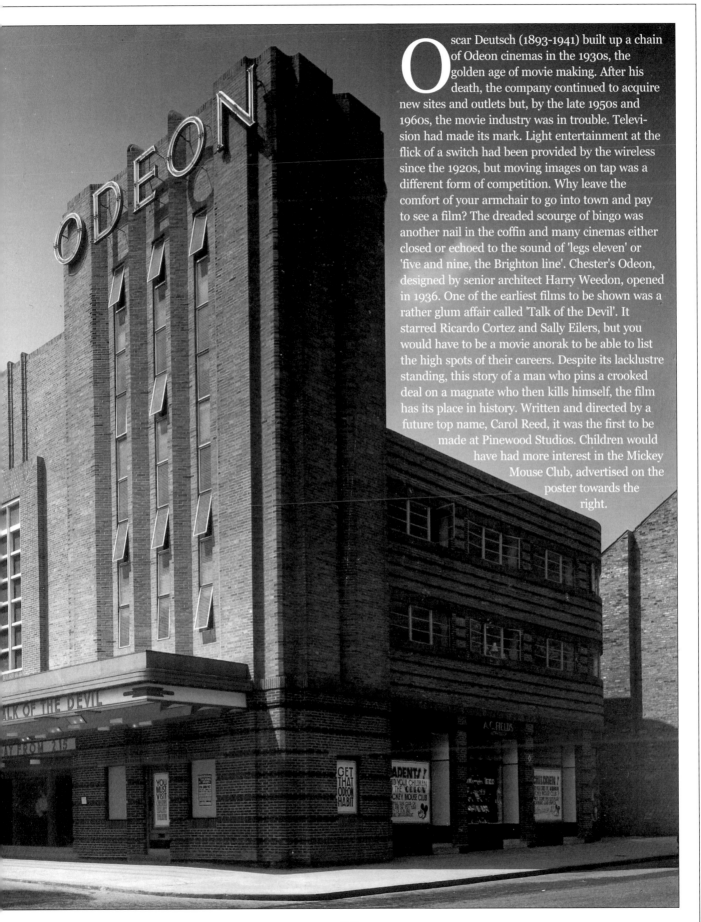

Oscar Deutsch (1893-1941) built up a chain of Odeon cinemas in the 1930s, the golden age of movie making. After his death, the company continued to acquire new sites and outlets but, by the late 1950s and 1960s, the movie industry was in trouble. Television had made its mark. Light entertainment at the flick of a switch had been provided by the wireless since the 1920s, but moving images on tap was a different form of competition. Why leave the comfort of your armchair to go into town and pay to see a film? The dreaded scourge of bingo was another nail in the coffin and many cinemas either closed or echoed to the sound of 'legs eleven' or 'five and nine, the Brighton line'. Chester's Odeon, designed by senior architect Harry Weedon, opened in 1936. One of the earliest films to be shown was a rather glum affair called 'Talk of the Devil'. It starred Ricardo Cortez and Sally Eilers, but you would have to be a movie anorak to be able to list the high spots of their careers. Despite its lacklustre standing, this story of a man who pins a crooked deal on a magnate who then kills himself, the film has its place in history. Written and directed by a future top name, Carol Reed, it was the first to be made at Pinewood Studios. Children would have had more interest in the Mickey Mouse Club, advertised on the poster towards the right.

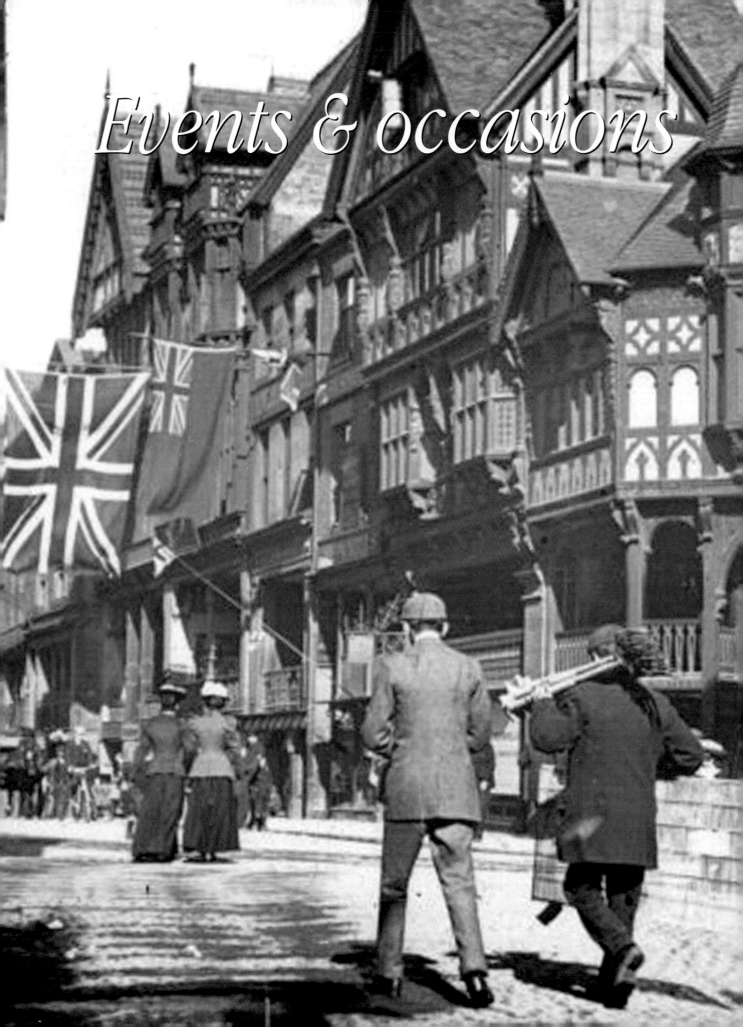

Events & occasions

Was the chimney sweep traversing The Cross off on a job or was he going to a wedding as a good luck charm? Looking from here to Eastgate Street, a handsome pair of women made their way past part of Chester's famous Rows. The fashion of the day dictated long sweeping skirts that modestly covered ankles, a glimpse of which could rouse all sorts of passions in men's breasts. The mind boggles as to the reaction that would greet the short skirts, crop tops and belly button adornments of the modern miss. Note the narrow waists favoured by our featured ladies. How much effort went into lacing and tightening corsets to enhance that effect is something at which we can only wonder. There must have been a fair amount of huffing and puffing, accompanied by sharp intakes of breath, before the women were ready to complete the process of getting dressed. It is little wonder that swooning was a common occurrence for ladies having to endure tight and heavy clothing in all temperatures. The photograph is undated, but must be associated with a royal event because of the union flags being flown. As fashion styles and modes of transport on view suggest that it was a century ago, perhaps we are witnessing part of the celebrations for the Coronation of Edward VII in August 1902. His son, George V, was crowned in June 1911 and that is another possibility, although by then cars would have been on the streets.

Above: Welcome home, lads. The flags of the world adorned the hall given over to a special party evening of thanks and celebration in honour of those who did us proud in World War II and had made it home to their loved ones from foreign fields as diverse as the European theatre of war, North Africa, Burma and Malaya. News that victory had been won in Europe was celebrated wildly on the streets in May 1945 and again, three months later, the crowds were out when victory over Japan was assured. However, especially in the former case, there was a limited number of soldiers, sailors or airmen at home at the time to join in the festivities. So, it was only right that a later date was set aside when the combatants could be feted in person. Even so, amidst the jollity of the occasion, glasses were raised in memory of those who had not made it. Women shed a quiet tear for the sweetheart or father who would not be coming home. For each one who had looked forward to the day she would be reunited with her husband, there was another who knew that hers lay in a foxhole or at the bottom of the sea. The men in the room took time out to remember the pals who set out on bombing raids over Hamburg: they had slept in bunks alongside theirs, but one night had scrambled at nine and were gone before dawn.

Below: The Town Hall on Market Square, Northgate Street is always the focus for official ceremonies and proclamations. Two flights of steps take visitors up to the main entrance where Chester's former armorial bearings are carved above the double doors. The present building was designed by Belfast architect William H Lynn who was selected for the job by way of a public competition. The central tower stands at a height of almost 50m above the gothic styled, sandstone symbol of the city's authority. The previous town hall, known as the Exchange, was built in the 17th century, but was consumed by fire in 1862. The main council chamber was also fire damaged in 1897, the year of Queen Victoria's diamond jubilee, and was restored the following year by TM Lockwood. In September 1948 dignitaries, who included the Mayor of Chester and Colonel GP Harding, took the salute from the 1st Battalion of the Cheshire Regiment under the command of Major FJ Gold. The parade included the 7th Battalion of the Cheshire Territorial Army and representatives from the Old Comrades Association and Cheshire County Cadets. Special permission had to be granted to allow the soldiers to parade through the city with their bayonets fixed. Two Cheshire Regiment flags can be seen above the doors into the Town Hall's Assembly Room.

Above: Princess Elizabeth was as popular as a movie matinee idol in April 1951. She was just approaching her 25th birthday and had a glamour that enhanced her position as heir to the throne. This made her popular with young men who admired her looks and even older stuffed shirts were heard to comment that they admired 'the cut of her jib'. Girls loved to imagine themselves in her role, decked out in the best that money could buy, and older women admired her as a princess able to combine her royal with those of being a wife and mother of two young children. As her motorcade swept down Bridge Street, no one was too worried about security. The thought that some lunatic might attack her was a ludicrous idea and her adoring public pressed close to get a special glimpse of the woman who would one day be Queen. Princess Elizabeth had come to Chester on the royal train. The Mayor, Alderman PH Lawson and Cheshire's Lord Lieutenant, Lord Leverhulme greeted her at the station. Her Royal Highness had come to attend the passing out ceremony of 400 officer cadets on the polo grounds at Eaton Hall. Little did the Princess or the crowds realise, but in just over nine months' time the early death of her father, George VI, would elevate her to the throne.

Bottom left: Ooh Matron! How can anyone of a certain age not think of the 'Carry on' series of films when seeing a group of pretty nurses in their neatly starched uniforms? Directed by Gerald Thomas, the movies contained four with a definite medical theme, from 'Carry on Nurse', to a pair of 'Doctor' films and 'Carry on Matron'. The double entendre humour of the late 1950s to the early 1970s was ideally suited to playing doctors and nurses! Such lovelies as Shirley Eaton, Joan Sims, Barbara Windsor and Patsy Rowlands, often under the orders of Hattie Jacques, were subjected to the various attentions of Kenneth Williams, Jim Dale and Sid James. Dated now, perhaps, but fun at the time. For once, no one had eyes for our angels of mercy standing outside Chester Royal Infirmary. Union flags fluttered, hats were waved vigorously and three cheers loudly called for as the royal couple left after an official visit to the hospital. Despite the porter's arms being outstretched as a form of barrier, it was only a token example of crowd control. We knew how to behave ourselves in 1957. The public also knew its place, several steps away from the Queen, as demonstrated by her husband, the Duke of Edinburgh, who always walked with a bearing that suggested he was resigned to his fate, one pace behind.

Above: Chester's famous Eastgate clock is one of the city's best known landmarks. It stands on top of the present Eastgate that was built in 1769 and funded by Richard, Lord Grosvenor. The former medieval gate that stood here had retained parts of the original Roman arches, traces of which were uncovered during repairs made in the vicinity in 1972. The clock was erected as part of the celebrations and commemorations that recognised the long years of service given to the country by Queen Victoria. Her Diamond Jubilee is the only event of its type to have been seen in this country as the next longest serving monarch, George III, died nine months short of achieving that magic 60 year figure. Victoria came to the throne on 20 June 1837 and JB Joyce made the jubilee clock in her honour in 1897, the iron framework being to a design by John Douglas. Somewhat incongruously, it was not erected until two years later. The motorcade passing underneath the arches in October 1949 had come from the General Station and brought a most important personage to the city. Queen Elizabeth (1900-2002), wife of George VI, was here to inspect the officers and men of the Queen Bays Regiment at the Dale, Upton by Chester. Her drive through the city streets was an opportunity for the crowds to cheer the woman who had stood firm alongside her husband during the war when others might have run off to safety overseas.

Below: Little lads had knees over 50 years ago, but you would never think that they have in the modern age as they roam about in long trousers that were forbidden until they approached their teenage years back then. Permanently scabbed over because of a series of playground tumbles during lunchtime games of 30 a-side soccer, those knees proudly boasted that they belonged to a proper boy and not one who was a namby-pamby bookworm. The lads and their families on Talbot Street in this photograph from 2 June 1953 were getting ready for their party as part of the celebrations for Queen Elizabeth's big day as she became officially recognised as our head of state. Children really enjoyed themselves by getting into party spirit, particularly as they were growing up during the austerity era of postwar Britain when things were still tight and rationing not completely a thing of the past. Now parents and grandparents themselves, they can still recall the magic of the moment. Many retained the coronation mugs given to them at school and these occupied pride of place on the mantelpiece. On every one of those mementoes a picture of Queen Elizabeth gazed out at them, forever young. At the moment, the jury is still out on what sort of reception a similar, future image of a Queen Camilla will attract.

Above: Talbot Street is situated off Hoole Way, sandwiched between the fire station and the railway. This group of party goers was obviously photographed on 2 June 1953, the date of the Coronation of Queen Elizabeth II. Little terraced houses shared one thing with large company offices and town halls, as all were decked with flags and bunting ready to celebrate the feting of a new monarch. When the great day came streets were closed off and church halls and schoolrooms raided for their furniture. Trestle tables were dragged out into the roadway, moaning under the weight of Plates of sandwiches, freshly baked buns, jolly jellies and jugs of lemonade. Children dressed up like little kings and queens. Wind up gramophones were cranked to blare out hokey cokey music and long congas were danced on the cobblestones. The day dawned damp and cloudy, but that was a minor irritation. Nothing was going to get in the way of our enjoyment. Nearly 1,000,000 TV sets were sold in the preceding weeks to enable families to gather around the little, flickering black and white picture. They listened to the superb tones of Richard Dimbleby's voice describing the pageantry of it all. One of the lasting memories of the procession was the sight of Queen Salote of Tonga. Her huge frame and beaming face were a joy to behold as she waved wildly from an open carriage rapidly filling with rainwater.

Steeled for change

When Harry and James Summers decided to site the family's new steelworks on the Dee Marshes at Hawarden Bridge, they could not have known that they were starting a business that would span three centuries and still be World renowned even in the 21st Century's fiercely competitive global steel industry.

The family already had a thriving works at Stalybridge, Manchester, making clog irons, nails and galvanised steel sheets, started by Harry and James' father John Summers in the 1860's. John died in 1876 leaving the business to his sons. In 1895 Harry and James recommended the purchase of forty acres of Dee marshland to their four brothers to start production of galvanised steel sheet and negotiations were soon under way. The only building on the site at the time was the black and white half-timbered clubhouse of Chester Golf Club, which had links on part of the land bought for the new works. It became the site office while the golf course was moved towards Shotwick. John Summers and Sons were ultimately to buy 10,000 acres in the area at a cost of five shillings an acre.

The first Deeside galvanised sheets were produced in September 1896, 250 people using steam driven mills to make 600 tonnes a week from bars imported from America. At the time Deeside was agricultural and sparsely populated, Shotton being a small village on the opposite bank of the river, so the family had to build an industrial community as well as a

*Top: General Office 1908. **Above:** John Summers and Sons' new steelworks at Hawarden Bridge in 1897.*

steelworks. By the turn of the century the company was making 40,000 tonnes of galvanised sheet, mostly for export. One of the key factors in selecting the Deeside site was its water and rail links and proximity to Birkenhead and Liverpool ports.

In 1902 the Works began making its own steel in nine fifty-ton open-hearth furnaces and, with a bar mill, the first homemade products were made. Ingots were turned into bars, which in turn were put through a steam driven hand mill resembling a giant mangle.

As the red-hot sheets came out from between two rolls they were caught with tongs and passed back over the mill to handlers who fed them through the rolls again. This process was repeated until the right thickness was achieved. The work was hot and dusty and the smell of oil and grease heavy in the air. The men wore sailcloth aprons called brats to guard their legs, sweat towels around their necks and sturdy clogs. It was work only for the strong and experienced!

In less than a decade an area of low lying marshland had been transformed into a hive of industry while Shotton, little more than a hamlet when the Summers brothers made their first visit, became a boom town as terraces of houses were built for the workers who came to Deeside from all over the country. The company also conveyed 30 acres for the building of Garden City for steel workers and their families.

Above: This half-timbered house was the only building on the site bought by John Summers and Sons for new steel works in 1895. It was originally the home of the greenkeeper for the Chester Golf Club which had its course at Hawarden Bridge. When construction of the works started some of the links moved to Shotwick and managers used the house until becoming the Chemistry Laboratory in 1902. It later became the foundry offices and remained a landmark for travellers on the Wrexham-Bidston rail line until its demolition in 1981.
Below: Rolling steel sheets in the Mill, 1910.

In 1908 an imposing General Office was built on the banks of the Dee, modelled on Manchester's Midland Hotel, and even today it's terracotta and red brick never fails to impress visitors to the site.

By 1910 the workforce had grown to 3,000 and large quantities of galvanised sheet were being shipped from Liverpool to all over the World. The work was largely organised under a contract system, which precipitated a major dispute and a strike, one of only two in the Works history. During the strike it came to light that two men were paid thirty shillings a week to carry beer into the Works to quench the thirst of the men working in the mills. This practice was stopped and Summers agreed to the opening of two small breweries by William Blackham in the Top Yard area making non-alcoholic drinks.

biggest problem was the American depression that had made its way across the Atlantic to spread across Europe. It hit Shotton Works in 1931 and on the 24th April, 'Black Friday', the steelmaking operation was closed and 4,000 of the 6,000 employees were sacked. The finishing operations kept going with much reduced output. The steel industry has always been cyclical and two years later there was a return to former glory and a move from traditional hand rolling mills to modern continuous strip manufacture

Throughout the 1930s the Works installed ground-breaking technology and its 'Galvatite®' branded product established Shotton as a leader in the world galvanised sheet market and put it in a strong position to meet the needs of Britain at the outbreak of war in 1939. Over 2 million tonnes were produced and hundreds of thousands were supplied for Anderson garden air raid shelters and Morrison shelters. Some 2000 men enlisted for war service and their jobs were taken by women; in production departments their main role was to drive cranes.

The Summers' family decision to site their Works at Shotton Works proved vital in protecting it from aerial bombing. The Clwydian hills and low lying marshes made it very difficult for the Luftwaffe to attack and by the end of the war in 1945 not one bomb had hit the site.

When Harry Summers died at the end of the war he left behind one of the world's largest steelworks making 8,000 tonnes a week and employing 6,000 people. Even the new Labour Government's decision in 1945 to nationalise steel could not deter the Summer's family from making Shotton a fully integrated site, with coke ovens, blast furnaces, new open heart steel making facilities and a power station. There was a brief flirtation with nationalisation in 1951, but when the Conservatives returned to Government, Shotton Works was given back to John Summers and Sons. The 1950s were boom years for the steel industry and by 1957 the Shotton Works

The outbreak of war in 1914 created new uses for black and galvanised sheets with all 49 mills working at full capacity and by 1916 the Works was making 500,000 tonnes a year.

A second steelworks, with eight 70-75 ton furnaces tonnes and a second bar mill were in production within a year, freeing the company from its dependence on imported bars. The post war boom was followed by worldwide over production and a collapse in prices. Shotton Works decided to counteract the slump by focusing on higher quality products for the car industry and began a ten-year transition from the mid 1920s.

Radical changes were made to the whole process from steel making to finished sheet to ensure cleanliness of the highest order. Even a human hair left on the roll could spoil the product! Many experiments followed, with varying degrees of success and significant problems had to be overcome, but the

Top left: *An open hearth furnace is tapped, 1910.*
Far left: *Patent flattening of galvanised sheets, 1910.*
Above: *The Packing Shop, 1910.*

expansion programme had created the largest melting shop in Europe and 10,000 jobs. The Works hit its target of 1 million tonnes and set its sights on 2 million.

By 1965 one fifth of the 1.5 million tonnes a year was being coated through hot dipped galvanising, electro galvanising, plating, painting etc. The following year the Labour Party increased its 1964 majority and again began the process of nationalisation. On 28th July, 1967, John Summers and Sons, along with thirteen other steel companies, became the British Steel Corporation. They had a combined workforce of 270,000 people, 12,000 of whom were based at Shotton Works

Shotton Works' status as the premier coatings plant in the Corporation was further enhanced in 1972 with coil-to-coil lines for electro-zinc plating and plastic film laminating. £20 million was also invested in new computer controlled cold rolling operations and associated facilities to meet the increasing demand for coated products. The open hearth steel making operations made Shotton Works less competitive than those with Basic Oxygen Converters, a major problem when the Government announced a 10 year modernisation of the steel industry. The 'heavy end' iron and steel making

operations were to be closed by March 1980 with the loss of 6,500 jobs. The national steel strike called in December 1979 in protest at works closures, meant that the heavy end did not re-open after Christmas. From 1975 onwards British Steel Industry Ltd., along with the Welsh Development Agency,

Top: Curving corrugated galvanised sheets for shelters.
Above: The crew of No 17 Hand Rolling Mill in 1926.

County Council authorities and other support groups developed 375 acres of Corporation land adjacent to the Works, now the Deeside Industrial Park, to replace jobs lost through rationalisation.

Shotton's unmatched depth of experience in galvanising and coatings was recognised with £70 million worth of investment for new lines to meet the ever-growing demand for coated products, particularly in the construction and domestic appliance markets. A second coatings plant was built at a cost of £45 million , doubling the Works' coatings capacity to over 800,000 tonnes a year. Shotton was justifiably proclaimed 'the coatings centre of Europe'.

As the steel industry came out of the 1980's deep recession Shotton Works focused its activities on producing top quality products for the automotive, construction, consumer products and general engineering markets. By 1985 a second hot dip galvanising line (No 6) was nearing completion, just as operations in the coatings one department, originally known as the Marsh, ended after almost half a century. The No 6 line, costing £30 million, provided a facility to produce thinner, wider zinc and aluminium-zinc coated strip at 5 times the speed of the older lines.

In September 1988, the British Steel Corporation was privatised and became British Steel plc. Investment in new technology intensified and in 1989 a new £60 million coatings three complex, including an electro plating line was built to meet the extended corrosion resistance requirements demanded by the automotive companies. A year later a new paint coating line was commissioned and Shotton became the first works in Europe capable of coating 1 million tonnes of steel strip each year. End uses included wall and roof cladding, car body parts, domestic appliances, electrical switchgear and ducting. By this time all aspects of external and internal Quality Standards were being met and Shotton had built a worldwide reputation for service and product quality.

At the end of 1991 the Works introduced a Total Quality Performance (TQP) philosophy to build on its quality reputation. The second phase of TQP was a team working initiative on a works-wide scale. Shotton was the first site in British Steel to implement such a programme and it was a time of great change and major investment; not, this time, in plant and equipment, but in people. Several million pounds were spent on training and development, including team development.

Below: *Air raid preparedness using Shotton galvanised sheet.*

Although the steel industry remains notoriously cyclical, throughout the 1990s the emphasis on individual and team development was sustained, even during times of difficult trading conditions. Thus, in 1996 when the Works celebrated its centenary, Shotton was well placed to take advantage of any opportunities the coated products market had to offer. An Investor In People since 1995, Shotton Works has been recognised and received several awards through ISO, ISRS, the Wales Quality Award People Development Prize and Investors In Excellence in 2004.

In 1999 British Steel plc agreed a merger with Netherlands biggest steel producer, Hoogovens Koninklijke, to create a new company. Corus came into being in January, 2000 signalling a new era for coated products. Shotton Works became headquarters for a new Business Unit, Corus Colors, one of twenty in the company. Corus Colors has works in the UK, Netherlands, France, and Turkey .

Corus Colors recognised the need to align itself more closely with the construction market where there was more opportunity to add value to the products and services. The decision to move away from Automotive together with a rationalisation of the UK steel assets within Corus, resulted in the closure of 3 lines. To help offset some of the job losses that resulted from this and utilise the company's significant expertise in large scale manufacturing, a new business was set up in 2003 called Corus Living Solutions. Developed and based at Shotton Works, Corus Living Solutions designs and manufactures prefabricated living modules for the construction sector and has already won orders to build armed forces accommodation in the South of England.

Other key activities at Shotton Works designed to help deliver its long-term success are focused around the development of strong products and services which differentiate the business from others in the market.

A market leader in pre-finished steel

Steel has come a long way since its early use for corrugated roofing. It has evolved into painted (pre-finished) steel where a number of paint layers and treatments are applied in an automated and carefully controlled manufacturing process. Shotton Works has been a pioneer in this and over the course of the last forty years has developed technically leading products under the Colorcoat® brand to the point where they have replaced cement and masonry for industrial and many commercial buildings and been prominently used on major landmark buildings.

Until pre-finished steel coating technology emerged in the mid 1960s, the most common materials used for roofs and walls were asbestos cement and masonry. In the decade that followed, when the dangers of asbestos were highlighted, significant market development effort by British Steel Corporation, ensured that pre-finished steel manufactured at Shotton Works quickly replaced it.

Throughout the 1970s and 1980s, vast improvements were made to the manufacturing process at Shotton Works, increasing quality control, colour ranges and product functionality. By the mid 1980s pre-finished steel had officially come of

Top left: One of the first shift teams to operate under a works-wide team working programme, July 1995. Top right: Design team at work in the Product Development Centre, early 1970s. Left: The Ashorne Hill management colleague in Leamington Spa is a modular building from Corus Living Solutions, a new Business set up on the Shotton site in 2001. The building uses wall panels made from Colorcoat Celestia and HPS200 all manufactured by Corus at the Shotton site.

age as a well accepted material for a variety of applications and British Steel Corporation was the market leader.

Coupled with significant investment in manufacturing at Shotton Works, came the application of consumer marketing principles. These helped to build what Shotton Works could offer the construction market into more than just painted steel coils. Firstly the company registered Colorcoat® as a trademark and made it synonymous with high quality pre-finished steel products for roofs and walls.

Secondly, it set about convincing architects and building owners that pre-finished steel was the material of choice and had many benefits over other materials such as masonry and concrete. This was done by running seminars, improving the product quality and colour choice and publishing high quality information that showed designers how to design effectively with pre-finished steel. For Shotton Works it also meant setting up a dedicated design service called the Product Development Centre. Established in the late 1960s, this offered design support and prototyping facilities to demonstrate Colorcoat® products capabilities.

Thirdly, it set about developing unique products and services which could be branded and clearly distinguish British Steel from competitors. Colorcoat HP200®, a unique and superior performing product was launched in 1986 and four years later became the first pre-finished steel product in Europe to be offered with a guarantee. So confident were British Steel in the performance of the Colorcoat HP200® manufactured at Shotton Works, they were prepared to provide cover for it for up to 20 years.

This commitment to pushing forward the boundaries continued through the 1990s and into the new millennium with the launch of new technically leading products such as Colorcoat Celestia® and Colorcoat HPS200®, and the expansion of the Confidex® guarantee. By 2004 Colorcoat HPS200®, manufactured at Shotton Works, had

deservedly become the most frequently asked for pre-finished steel for roofs and walls in Europe.

Shotton Works has played an enormous role in the development of British Steel and latterly Corus position as a lead supplier to the construction market. Not only does it provide the very best manufacturing facilities and quality standards for Colorcoat® products, it also has enormous expertise built up over 40 years. This has been channelled into a dedicated help-line Colorcoat Connection® and a comprehensive Colorcoat® Building manual for architects. These provide advice and guidance on all design and construction aspects of pre-finished steel for roofs and walls and really help Corus to stand out in the market.

So what of the future for Shotton Works? Although the last 20 years have been turbulent for the site, it has remained at the forefront of coating technology and a lead supplier to the construction industry. And this will remain its focus moving forward. Being efficient and continued investment in new products and services that push the boundaries forward will remain important. With over 40 years experience in coating steel, Shotton Works can offer a level of expertise, knowledge and peace of mind that competitors find difficult to match. And building on this heritage and reputation as an innovator through the Colorcoat® brand will help ensure long-term success.

Top left: *Cardiff Millennium stadium using wall panels made from Colorcoat Celestia and HPS200.*
Below: *The Odyssey Arena using wall panels made from Colorcoat Celestia.*

Colorcoat, Colorcoat Connection, Colorcoat Building, Confidex,Celestia, HPS200, Galvatite and Living Solutions are trademarks of Corus

Wartime

Below left: War had been declared, and every citizen of Britain, young and old, male and female, was called upon to put his or her back into the war effort. Those who did not go into military service of one kind or another worked in factories, dug for victory, gave up their tin baths and aluminium saucepans, joined organisations and aided in any way they could. These boys were not going to be left out; they might be too young to fight but while there were sandbags to be filled they were going to do their bit to protect their school building. Thousands of sandbags were used during World War II to protect the country and its beautiful civic buildings.

Below: A proud father poses for the camera with his latest arrival. The baby had not arrived from Mars, in fact the 'arrival' was not a baby at all, but an anti-gas attack suit which was compulsory for babies in the United Kingdom during the Second World War. An air pump at the side of the suit enabled anxious parents to replenish the supply of air to the precious package inside. It is said that most babies were less than enthusiastic abut the prospect of being encased in the suit - and who could blame them? The picture was taken in 1939. In the event there was never any gas attack on British soil during the course of the Second World War.

In 1939 Britain's Prime Minister Neville Chamberlain had made his announcement to the waiting people of Britain that '...this country is at war with Germany.' The country rolled up its sleeves and prepared for the inevitable. This war would be different from other wars. This time planes had the ability to fly further and carry a heavier load, and air raids were fully expected. Air raid shelters were obviously going to be needed, and shelters were built on open places across towns and cities. By the time war was declared an army of volunteers of both sexes had already been recruited to form an Air Raid Protection service. At first ARP personnel were unpaid volunteers but when war broke out in September 1939 they became paid staff. It was their job to patrol specified areas, making sure that no chinks of light broke the blackout restrictions, checking the safety of local residents, being alert for gas attacks, air raids and unexploded bombs. The exceptional work done by Air Raid Wardens in dealing with incendiaries, giving first aid to the injured, helping to rescue victims from their bombed-out properties, clearing away rubble, and a thousand and one other tasks became legendary; during the second world war nearly as many private citizens were killed as troops - and many of them were the gallant ARP wardens. At the beginning of the war Sir Anthony Eden, Secretary of State for War, appealed in a radio broadcast for men between 17 and 65 to make up a new force, the Local Defence Volunteers, to guard vulnerable points from possible Nazi attack. Within a very short time the first men were putting their names down. At first the new force had to improvise; there were no weapons to spare and men had to rely on sticks, shotguns handed in by local people, and on sheer determination . Weapons and uniforms did not become available for several months. In July the Local Defence Volunteers was renamed the Home Guard, and by the following year was a force to be reckoned with. Television programmes such as 'Dad's Army' have unfortunately associated the Home Guard with comedy, but in fact they performed much important work. The Guard posted sentries to watch for possible aircraft or parachute landings at likely spots such as disused aerodromes, golf courses

on the outskirts of towns, local parks and racecourses. They manned anti-aircraft guns, liaised with other units and with regular troops, set up communications and organised balloon barrages. Other preparations were hastily made. Place names and other identifying marks were obliterated to confuse the enemy about exactly where they were. Notices went up everywhere giving good advice to citizens on a number of issues. 'Keep Mum - she's not so dumb' warned people to take care what kind of information they passed on, as the person they were speaking to could be an enemy.

Older readers will remember how difficult it was to find certain items in the shops during the war; combs, soap, cosmetics, hairgrips, elastic, buttons, zips - all were virtually impossible to buy as factories that once produced these items had been turned over to war work. Stockings were in short supply, and resourceful women resorted to colouring their legs with gravy browning or with a mixture of sand and water. Beetroot juice was found to be a good substitute for lipstick.

Clothes rationing was introduced in 1941, and everyone had 66 coupons per year. Eleven coupons would buy a dress, and sixteen were needed for a coat. The number of coupons was later reduced to 40 per person. People were required to save material where they could - ladies' hemlines went up considerably, and skirts were not allowed to have lots of pleats. Some found clever ways around the regulations by using materials that were not rationed. Blackout material could be embroidered and made into blouses or skirts, and dyed sugar sacks were turned into curtains.

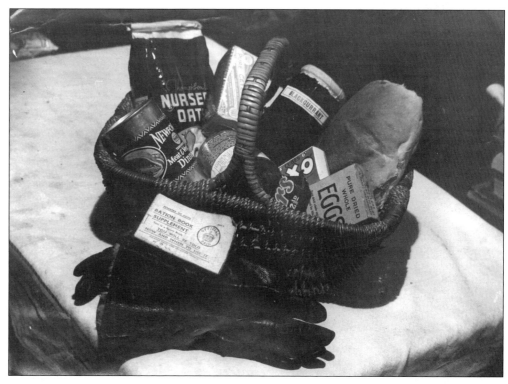

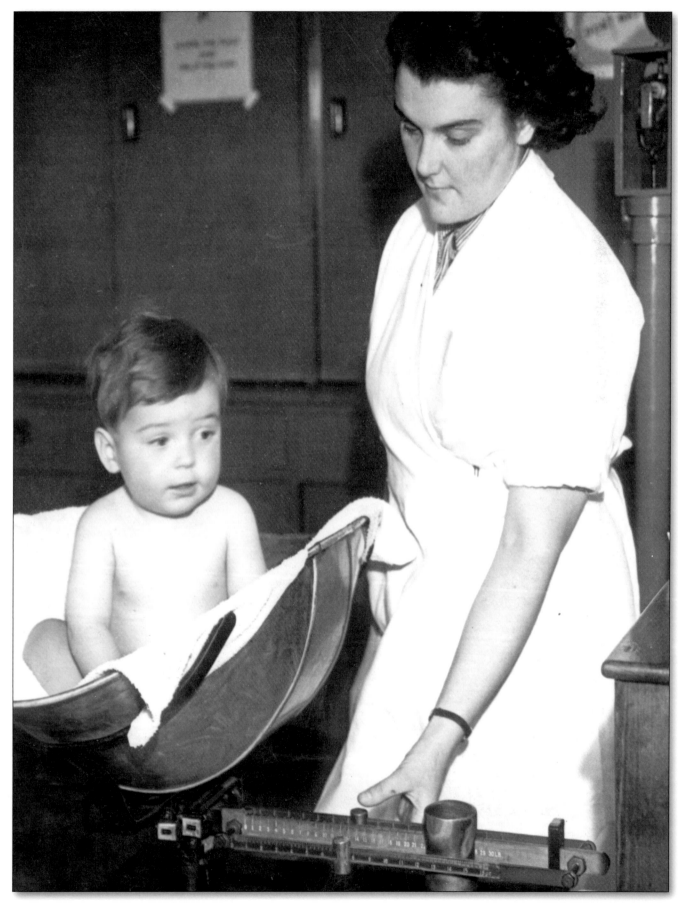

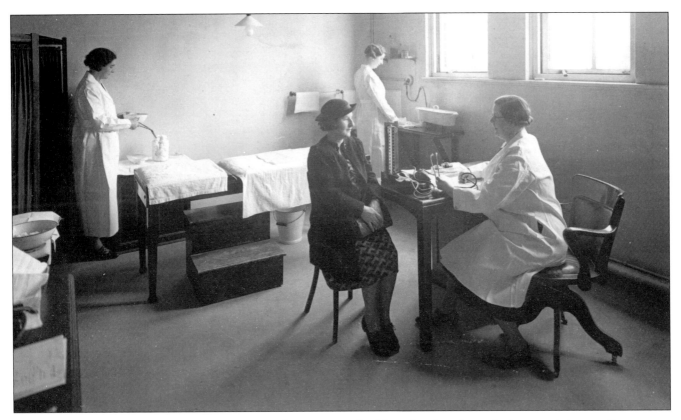

Both pages: It was possibly the acute wartime shortages of food and supplies which made doctors, health workers and mothers alike very aware of the health of the new generation, and children were carefully weighed, measured and immunised against the illnesses that had at one time meant disfigurement or even death *(facing page)*. A vaccine for polio, the scourge of former years which left behind its terrible mark of wasted and useless limbs, only came later, however. American scientist Jonas Edward Salk developed a vaccine in 1955, and an oral vaccine was produced in 1960. The vaccines brought the dreaded disease under control and today polio is rarely seen. On a day to day basis, vitamins were vital to the health of children, and long before the advent of the cod liver oil capsule, the recommended spoonful of cod liver oil was administered to the youngest children every day in schools and nurseries around the country during the 1940s. Children might have screwed up their noses at the fishy taste, but the nourishing cod liver oil went a long way towards keeping them

healthy. The vitamin-packed orange juice was far more palatable, and artful mothers would often use the orange juice as a bribe: no cod liver oil, no orange juice. Following hard on the heels of the oil, the juice took away the distinctive taste that was disliked by so many children. Ante-natal clinics did all they could to check on the diet, blood pressure and vitamin intake of mothers to be; our carefully posed photograph *(top)*, taken in an ante-natal clinic in the 1930s, records at least the cleanliness and tidiness that was to their great credit. And when the tiny new citizen finally arrived, there were health visitors to pay friendly calls on families in their homes to check on

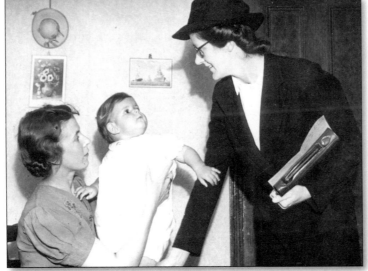

the health and happiness of mothers and babies *(left)*. National Dried Milk for babies was also made available to mothers, and before today's push towards natural feeding NDM was for decades very much in vogue. We need to remember that at the time of these photographs the National Health service did not exist, and in fact the NHS only came into operation after World War II in July 1948.

Shopping spree

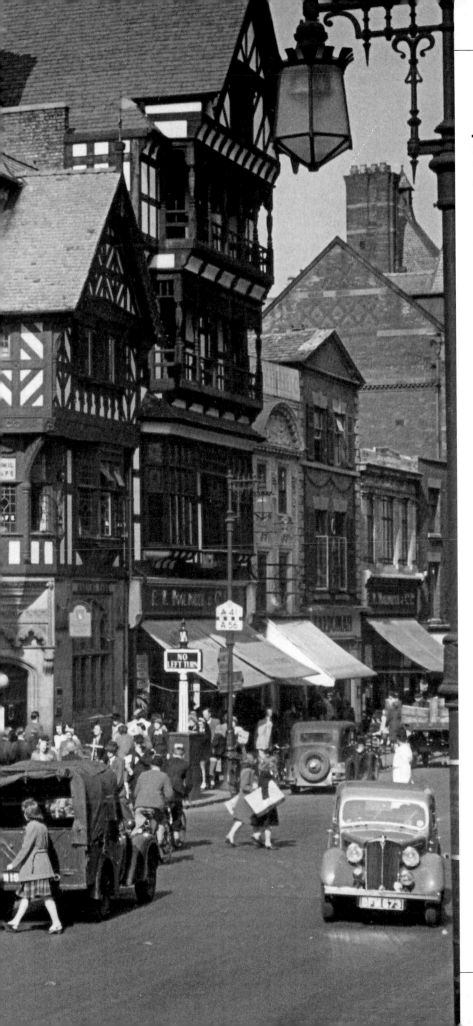

A summer day on Eastgate Street in 1948 meant that shoppers, visitors and office workers were out in force as the sun shone brightly upon them. Pretty girls in short sleeved blouses or neatly tailored suits with a divided skirt took the eye. The younger generation, many great grandmas by now, was a more daring one than its predecessor, just as it is today. In the 21st century, young women bare their midriffs, adorn them with small tattoos and attach gold studs to their navels. Their mothers, and definitely their fathers, usually disapprove. Nearly 60 years earlier, that same level of disapproval was directed at young women daring to go out and about bare headed. That was decidedly infra dig and not a good example of how they had been raised! Tut tut, indeed. You could probably blame it on the influence of those Yanks who were here during the war, with their happy go lucky ways and no sense of dignity or decorum. Some things American, though, had long been accepted into our way of life. To the right of the photograph, near the policeman on point duty, we can see FW Woolworth's. The original five and ten cent store, with its cheap and cheerful goods and shopgirls who never seemed to know the price of the items they sold, had been around since the first British outlet opened in Liverpool before the first world war.

Below: Even the cyclists have come to a halt in Eastgate Street's congestion, typical of the rush hour scene on our roads even as far back as 1951. Normally, two wheels could nip in and out of the lines of stationary cars, but the bottleneck was so bad on this occasion that even the budding Reg Harrises or future Beryl Burton on view had come to a halt. Cycling was both a popular pastime and much used mode of transport in the early postwar years. Cars and fuel were expensive and beyond the reach of the ordinary person's pay packet. During those austere years, most of us had a keen eye for a bargain. Something seems to have caught the attention of the leading cyclist because he has swivelled his neck through about 125 degrees. It could be the narrow waisted lady in the floral print dress that has taken his eye, but it could also be the possibility of the bargain price clothing on sale at the Fifty Shilling Tailor. This company, a common sight on most high streets in England either side of the war, was founded by Leeds' Henry Price (1877-1963). He acknowledged that, despite money being tight, men still wanted to dress as elegantly as they could afford and he spotted a niche in the market. So, he established his chain, selling cheap but acceptable clothing. Soon he had a string of stores across the country that remained popular throughout the 1950s until greater prosperity and a desire for more fashionable clothing altered purchasing patterns. Price was knighted in 1937 and, after his passing, left a legacy of fond memories of the days when his suits cost just £2.50, in today's terminology.

Right: In the immediate postwar years Britain was under the control of Clement Attlee's Labour government that swept to power in a landslide victory in the summer of 1945. Voters gave thanks for all Mr Churchill had done for them during the war, but 'No thanks' when it came to peacetime. The public wanted no more of the old and looked for an Aladdin to bring it the new lamps of the future. Unfortunately, Mr Attlee did not turn out to be the genie for which it hoped. Despite the success of educational and medical reforms, the economy lurched along disappointingly. Our country's finances were mortgaged to the hilt and we had to rely on the Marshall Aid plan from America to help make ends meet. No more would Britain be a super power as we became committed to being a form of Yankee puppet. The country's monetary situation was such that the pound was devalued by 30 per

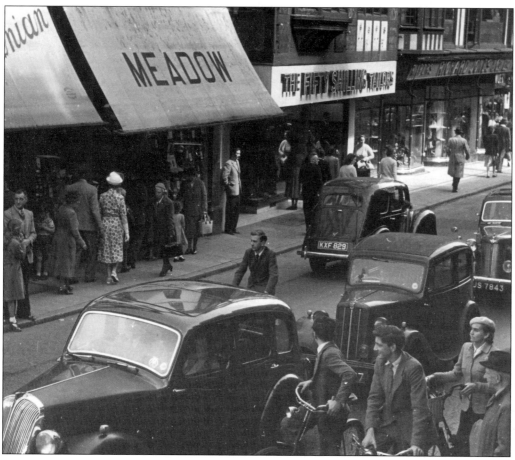

cent in August 1949. Yet, to look at Eastgate Street in 1951, things did not seem too bad. Shoppers were out in force and cars crowded the highway. But behind the façade of affluence illustrated in this photograph, lurked an austerity that still hurt. The range of goods in the shops was limited and expensive. Meat was still rationed, even six years after the end of the war, and was limited to a quarter of a pound of beefsteak per person per week. Voters turned back to Churchill in the general election a few months after this picture was taken.

Left: 'Aye-aye, that's your lot', as Jimmy Wheeler, a popular comedian of this photograph's era, might have put it, even if the first little part of his catchphrase would have to be re-spelt to fit with the sign above Siddall's shop on Bridge Street. In 1948 this outlet, established in 1815, doubled as an optician and umbrella maker. That quirky combination of trades could have provided comics with material for a joke or two. Like Jimmy Wheeler, many of them had catchphrases that they trotted out regularly. Ken Platt would inform us that 'I won't take my coat off, I'm not stopping', Al Read often commented 'Right, monkey' and Sandy Powell asked 'Can you hear me mother?' But it would be Arthur Askey who would feel at home here with his particular favourite of 'Before your very eyes'. The other shops pictured along here included Shaw's ironmongers, Jefferson's drapery, the English Leather Company, Willerby's tailors and Marston's cycle shop. Shoppers were obviously out in force under the Rows as the world they knew was changing about them. The spectre of communism hung like a pall that Winston Churchill described as an 'iron curtain' and soon 'reds under the beds' scares and the threat posed by nuclear weapons came to haunt them. Most of the shops on view changed hands, but Siddall's survived into the new millennium.

Below: The pedestrians going over the road at the Belisha crossing in August 1951 were using one of the clutch of road safety innovations introduced in the mid 1930s. Before the war, the number of deaths and serious accidents on the roads provided statistics that were among the worst in Europe. The Highway Code was issued, offering good advice and instructions to all road users. Electrically operated traffic lights became the norm at busy junctions, cats' eyes marked the roads and specially trained traffic police enforced urban speed restrictions. It seems remarkable to us now that anyone could get behind the wheel until the mid 1930s, as it was only then that the driving test was introduced. Pedestrians were given some consideration by Leslie Hore-Belisha, the Minister for Transport (1934-37). The crossings and beacons that bear his name gave the public some protection, though it took a while before people got used to them. The famous black and white 'zebra' markings were not used until later in 1951, following car drivers' complaints that they often failed to spot the road studs until too late. Many of the names on the shops we can see are no more and the line of rabbits hanging out on the street outside the butcher's is a definite thing of the past, but the face of the Rows lives on.

Above: The shop fronts may have been modernised and the names above the doors changed over the last 50 years, but little about the architectural face of this top end of Bridge Street has altered in the intervening years. The square face of St Peter's Church continues to dominate the scene. This place of worship, though not unique, is quite unusual in that it does not possess a nave, the long narrow central hall that rises higher than the aisles flanking it that is a feature of most cruciform churches. The origins of St Peter's probably date back to Saxon times, though the interior is about 600 years old. The church was heavily restored in 1887 and is often used for services by the Freemen and Guilds of Chester. Some of the streets leading off Bridge Street have interesting connections. Feathers Lane, just to the right of where the photographer was standing, led to the site of the former Feathers Hotel, a premier coaching inn. The Grosvenor Precinct has now swallowed up this street. Over the cameraman's left shoulder, White Friars is still with us. This street reminds of the monastery built by the Carmelites in 1277. These white robed monks belonged to one of the four great mendicants whose origins can be traced to Berthold, a Crusader who founded the Order on Mount Carmel in Palestine in 1155.

Right: The photographer was perched on the city walls at Eastgate to capture this view along Eastgate Street, beyond The Cross and on towards St Peter's Church and the start of Watergate Street. The Cross is a major feature of Chester's history as this is where merchants traded and struck their deals from the early 15th century until the middle of the 17th century. These activities took place around the High Cross. However, this monument would not have been visible in this picture as it spent many years in the Roman Gardens next to the Newgate, before being re-erected in 1975. The city's town crier makes his appearance here on most days of the week during the spring and summer months, making announcements following his traditional cry of 'Oyez'. The crier also carries the title of city beadle, a name that conjures up images of Oliver Twist and Mr Bumble. Now just an honorary role, beadles in earlier times performed functions similar to those carried out by parish officers responsible for keeping the unruly in order. In this photograph, probably from c1960, the usual crowds were out in force. There seldom seems to be quiet a time on our city streets, one of the problems of being such a popular and attractive venue for visitors from all over the world.

Bird's eye view

The swinging 60s brought us greater prosperity and a decade in which the under 25s became important figures in the economy and on the fashion and leisure fronts. They also had influence on attitudes towards morality and the rights of minorities. Young people, the product of the wartime and baby boomer years, had money in their pockets and a voice to be heard. They did not want to be little clones of their parents, but individuals in their own right. Men's hair descended at the same rate that girls' hemlines rose. Greater tolerance was shown to minority groups and vociferous objections raised against war mongerers and the nuclear threat. 'Make love not war, baby' as flowers were stuck down soldiers' gun barrels. The Pill provided an easy solution to the restrictions imposed by parental moral codes and the old order felt threatened by the rise in influence of those it felt were wet behind the ears. Sweeping changes were afoot as the faces of our towns and cities were altered. In Chester, in the mid 1960s, the sweeping arc of the inner ring road from the Northgate roundabout to St Martin's Gate was well on its way to completion. Its creation was a necessary eyesore designed to protect the centre of the city from interminable traffic problems. To the right, we can see a reminder of the days when transport was a much gentler and slower operation. The Shropshire Union Canal, with its staircase of three locks at the bottom of the picture, evokes memories of the days when horsepower meant just that.

Working life

During the second world war women worked long hours doing more than their bit for the country. At the Anchor Motor Company they fulfilled many of the roles that had been vacated by the men who had answered the nation's call to arms. This firm performed an important function at its premises on Grosvenor Street and Pepper Street, with additional workshops on Park Street where these women diligently worked upon the aircraft wings that would soon be airborne in the defence of our realm against the Luftwaffe's bombing raids on our cities. Scraping off the old fabric was hard, laborious work, but the women attacked the frames with a will, knowing that their efforts would of benefit to the war effort. When they got home after a long shift, they scrubbed hard and washed themselves vigorously to try to remove the dirt and grime of the job and get rid of the pervading fishy smell of the adhesives used to reattach the new fabric. When all that was done, there was a home to be run. Meals for the children needed cooking, the washing done and the house cleaned. Some even then went on to voluntary service as part of the civil defence in their so-called spare moments. To think they are referred to as 'the weaker sex'.

Below: In Britain the Christmas season begins in the summer. That is an indisputable fact, drawn from evidence in our 21st century shops as goods with an eye on the festive period are on sale earlier and earlier with every passing decade. Nowadays, no Christmas is complete without vast fortunes being spent on presents, food, drink and a host of other goodies that we really do not need. Credit cards melt with overuse and bank balances go into the red at an alarming rate, leaving the finance companies that pretend to save families money by consolidating debts, rubbing their hands with glee. A wartime Christmas was a far cry from the greed and spendthrift attitudes that abound today. Even basic commodities were in short supply and even icing was banned on cakes. Turkeys and geese did not adorn the table as families were lucky to get a scrawny chicken to share. Presents were mainly homemade, with little dolls being whittled from a piece of wood, and toy cars put together from bits of scrap metal dad had been able to scrounge from somewhere and then carefully shape with his own handtools. Decorations were sparse, but cleverly made from painted bits of old newspaper. The workforce at the Anchor Motor Company sat down en masse for its modest Christmas lunch. There were more patriotic flags on show than streamers, and the fare may have been plain, but the enjoyment and camaraderie was real, nonetheless.

Above: This group of workmen can possibly claim to be Old Boys of the grammar school at Queens Park. After all, they helped on this building project, putting just as much effort into their work as any inky fingered schoolboy sweating over his Latin primer. Taking a well earned rest from the strenuous manual labour that was involved, as the amount of supportive machinery available to them was of a limited nature, these workmen belonged to a class structure that had very clearly defined lines in the early 20th century. Even their clothing had a uniformity that shouted out their station in life. With just one exception, perhaps because he was one of the younger members of the gang and something of a renegade, they all wore almost identical flat caps. In modern times, of course, that headgear would still be of a uniform variety, but it would be of the safety conscious Bob the Builder yellow hardhat variety. Looking at our workforce in this photograph, it is interesting to note that the similarity of clothing is not just limited to the caps. Nearly all of the men are wearing jackets, with our rebel sporting a waistcoat, just to be different. But even this individual is sporting a necktie, just like the others who have either a tie or muffler around their necks.

The British war machine has won many famous victories and fought countless glorious campaigns down the years. Sea power and nautical skills determined the triumph at Trafalgar in 1805. Infantry and artillery forces won the day at Waterloo in 1815 and who has not heard of the cavalry charge of the Light Brigade at Balaclava in 1854? But, military styles evolve with time and advances in technology. The first world war began with men in trenches being assailed by machine guns and heavy artillery, but ended with tanks rolling across the plains and aircraft involved in dogfights in the skies above. By the time that World War Two broke out, it was obvious that air supremacy was to be the keynote.

Evidence of the influence of the aeroplane as a combat machine was drawn from the Spanish Civil War of 1936-39. Production at the Anchor Motor Company was quickly transferred from road machines to those ready to take to the skies. The largely female workforce is seen here fitting out cockpits. These women quickly garnished a wide range of technical skills to equip them for their work. All over the country, women took the places that the men left behind. They operated heavy plant in factories, welded metal in engineering workshops, drove tractors on the fields and brought in the harvest. They also raised the next generation.

Above: Transport needs and demands altered after World War Two as, gradually and then with a gallop, the car became king. Bus and train services that once had a monopoly were increasingly challenged by the use of the motorcar in everyday life as private ownership became the norm rather than the exception. Travel to and from work and leisure activities shifted away from public transport. This increased pressure on roads and town centres, required transport and highway strategies to be reviewed. Ring roads and bypasses were built and traffic flow measures such as parking restrictions, one way systems and pedestrianisation were pressed into service. In November 1964, seen from Canal Street, the new flyover was taking shape. Plans for a ring road were drawn up just after the war, but mothballed for two decades. The placement of the concrete pillars that would support the flyover and the new road itself meant that many fine, old buildings were swept away in the name of progress. At this time Dr Beeching was making his unpopular rail cuts, putting more pressure on the roads. By 1970, only the General Station remained as the axe fell on Northgate and Liverpool Road Stations.

Below: Surely there is an obvious candidate for a title caption that can be given to this photograph. It just has to be 'Up on the Roof', a major hit song for the Drifters in America, with cover versions by Kenny Lynch and Julie Grant doing well in Britain in the early 1960s. Robson and Jerome, somewhat less tunefully, took the song to the top of the charts in 1995. From the look of their clothing and hairstyles, this quintet of fresh faced, young ladies would have more in common with the original version of the song than that recorded by a pair of squawking actors. The girls experienced the fun that was Britain in the swinging 60s and were doubtlessly discussing the respective merits of boutique fashions and the mophead haircuts of a certain Fab Four from Liverpool. They were enjoying the view from the roof of the North West Securities (NWS) House on City Road that opened in June 1963 as the Beatles enjoyed their first No 1 with 'From me to you'. The Mayor of Chester, Councillor T Sarl-Williams, performed the official ceremony. NWS had its origins in a motor garage group that set up a loan company in 1945 to aid car purchase on tick. In 1997 the company became the Capital Bank and started to ask 'What's in your wallet?'

Applied education built on tradition: Chester's University

Founded by the Church of England in 1839 Chester College, now a University, was opened by W.E Gladstone as the first purpose-built teacher training College in the country.

In the early days, the trainees would have worn distinctive uniforms, eaten with the lecturers in the refectory and would followed a strict code of conduct. It's difficult to believe now that two students were investigated for entering an inn in 1841. This was strictly forbidden for young aspiring school masters.

However in the spirit of this book which is about living memory, the post war years and, particularly the last twenty, have been revolutionary not least in terms of the appearance of the College. Passing through on the A540, you will see quite clearly a Victorian facade and a fine chapel but, on entry, the landscape reflects these changes in appearance.

Bordered by three modes of transport, the Shropshire Union Canal, the railway and the Parkgate Road, the nucleus of the College has moved from the Victorian Old College and Chapel towards the white brick buildings and enhanced sports facilities to the South of the campus. The reason for this change in physical profile was an influx of public money into the higher education sector and Chester's desire to diversify. From an institution with a high reputation for the training of teachers, the College moved towards a widening of its curriculum to reflect the needs of other employers and the local community. The archives tell us that the College's first intake in 1841 was 45 students. More significantly in 1989 (the 150th year there were 1100) and now there are 11,000 people studying on campus.

The growth of the College has also meant a breathing of new life into historic buildings in Chester. Feathers Lane (opposite Owen Owens) for example had become a cause for concern for many local residents. Now the Victorian court buildings have been converted into student accommodation. The Grade One Listed Bluecoat School in Northgate Street, founded by the Bishop of Chester in 1717 has maintained its tradition of education through the habitation of the College's History Department who are now working with the Council's Heritage Services to improve access to local history and archaeology. Even the clock has been refurbished!

One aspect of College life has not changed. Even after this expansion, past and present students still talk of the "community atmosphere" and the "caring ethos." More recently this became more formalised with the establishment of Student Guidance and Support Services but the mission to educate people for the real needs of society has not changed since College bells first chimed in the very first intake.

The College, which now enjoys full university status, has a right to be nostalgic about its past. The tremendous turn out of the thriving post war reunion groups who frequent campus at weekends is clear testament to that. (The College Association has at least 8 ,000 active members aged from 21 to 101) But it is very much looking forward to building on its long and distinguished history as part of the country's higher education system.

Above: *Chester Diocesan Training College, with Chapel and National School, from an early lithograph in 1847.*
Below: *The College has a long tradition of sporting success. This is the College football team of 1889.*

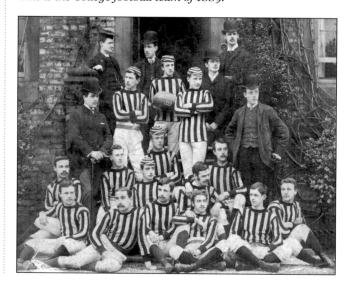

Third generation still going strong

It was in the dark days of post-war 1947 that Edgar Maltby set up his furniture business in a small shop in Brooke Street. Edgar had worked as a cabinet maker for what was known as the Stag Furniture Company. He eventually decided to go it alone and make his dreams a reality, a shop of his own!

In 1965, Edgar's son Maurice took over the running of the Company. Trained and time served in the furniture trade with Richard Jones (known as Owen Owen's) he was ideally suited to take on this Company. Maurice soon bought the neighbouring premises, and in 1982 when the local butchers, Baker and Gale closed he took that building too to create one of the largest retail frontages in Chester. When greengrocer Jacky Barlow subsequently retired, Maurice also bought his shop.

During this time, Chris Maltby joined the family firm after first completing his A-levels, he then went to Northampton College to undertake a Business & Finance degree. He spent a year at 'Brintons' one of Britain's foremost carpet manufacturers based in Kidderminster to learn at first hand the complete manufacturing process from fleece to the finished product, a carpet!

Sadly in 1994 Maurice passed away, leaving his son Christopher to run the third generation of Maltby's.

Chris his wife Sally and sister Anna together with the help of their superb staff are committed to preserving the same family principles that Edgar and Maurice always valued. 'Maltby's' reputation and service levels are of paramount importance, to remain committed to providing high quality products, a great service, for the best value at all times.

Maltby's is best known for its spectacular displays of floorcoverings. Offering advice that you can trust, professional planning and installation from their carpet fitters. When it comes to choice look no further! Solid wood floors, laminates, vinyls, karndean, coir and sisal and their

speciality carpets. With access to thousands of carpet samples in a myriad of colours and shades, even special dyes! Patterns or plains you will be spoilt by their elaborate displays from famous top quality carpets at affordable prices.

You will also find an array of home furnishings. Whether you are looking for timeless traditionality to classic elegance or a contemporary twist, from fireside chairs, comfortable suites, fine furniture, impressive beds and bedroom furniture to create the room of your dreams.

Maltby's client base comes from far and wide, from small town houses, flats and country cottages right through to some of Cheshire's best known hotels and stately homes, famous footballers, Lords and Ladies, Barons and Baronesses!

Recommendation is the Company's biggest source of work and they value their customers whoever they may be, no matter how big or small a job, everyone at Maltby's cares.

This family business has enjoyed a well deserved reputation for quality and an uncompromising attitude for a personal service for nearly sixty years.

Top left: Edgar Maltby, founder.
Above: Maurice Maltby, son of Edgar who took over the business in 1965. **Below:** Maltby's Brook Street premises pictured in 1997.

The Queen of schools

Since the introduction of education league tables Chester's Queen's School has consistently appeared as the top school in Cheshire. It continues to keep abreast of developments in education, maintaining its high standards of education across all fields - academic, sport, music and drama - whilst also expanding its extra-curricular programme.

A meeting of Chester dignitaries, amongst whom were the Bishop and the Dean, was held in November 1877 'for the purpose of establishing a school for the education of the daughters of the Middle Classes'. Until that time, secondary education for girls in

Above: The front of The Queen's School, 1910.
Below: The Upper 11 with Miss Polard in 1913.

Chester had been available at the Convent School founded in 1854, and at a number of privately run 'ladies schools' within the city boundaries.

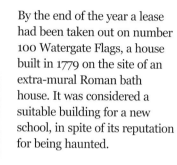

By the end of the year a lease had been taken out on number 100 Watergate Flags, a house built in 1779 on the site of an extra-mural Roman bath house. It was considered a suitable building for a new school, in spite of its reputation for being haunted.

The Chester School for Girls was formally opened on 1st May 1878 with an intake of sixteen pupils ranging from eight to sixteen years old. The first headmistress, Miss Constance Holdich, who initially undertook to run the school single-handed, sorted the girls into three classes. She was much impressed by the docility of Chester girls in comparison

The house was purchased with the help of Mrs Phyllis Brown, a member of the family who founded 'Browns of Chester', and who was vice-chairman of the Board of Governors.

Number 57 Liverpool Road was bought in 1946, and in 1961 the adjoining property also. These attractive Victorian houses, now re-named after former headmistresses Miss Sandford and Miss Nedham, are where the present Lower School is based.

with London girls. Within six months, the number of students had risen to sixty, with fees of £10, £8 or £6, according to age.

The city gaol, situated between the Royal Infirmary and Stanley Place, was closed in 1872, and the land it stood on was acquired by the first Duke of Westminster, who then offered the land to the rapidly expanding school for the erection of a new building. Designed by AE Ould of Newgate Street, the new school was constructed of red brick in the Tudor Gothic style.

On March 7th 1883, precisely one year after laying the foundation stone, the Duke of Westminster officially opened the school. At this point, it was still known as the Chester School for Girls, but after being approached by the Duke of Westminster, Queen Victoria commanded 'that the school in question shall be styled the 'Queen's School'.

Boarders had been admitted as early as the 1880s, and were lodged in nearby houses; in 1907 however, the boarders were moved to the north wing of the school, which continued in full use until 1941. It was eventually closed because of the risk of air raids during the second world war, coupled with the need for more classrooms, and was never re-opened.

In October 1887 arrangements were made for the admission of a class of very young girls, it was not however until 1932 that 7 Stanley Place was bought to provide separate accommodation for the preparatory department.

Following the 1944 Education Act, application was successfully made to the Minister of Education for the school to become a direct grant grammar school. That status was maintained until 1976 when the phasing out of the system was begun, and the school became fully independent once again.

In more recent times the neighbouring City Walls Hotel was bought and converted into a learning resource centre on the ground floor, and sixth form facilities on the second two floors; girls have showers, cloakrooms and common rooms, one for each of the two sixth form years. Opened by the Duchess of Gloucester, the former hotel was renamed MacLean House after a previous head, Miss MacLean, whose legacy enabled the school to purchase the hotel. Other major developments, building works and refurbishments continue unabated.

Since it was founded the Queen's School has acquired an enviable and well deserved reputation for academic excellence; it has undergone many changes, but it still remains committed to providing an outstanding education for girls.

Top left: Commemoration Service in Chester Cathedral in May 1963. *Top right:* The new entrance opened in January 2003. *Left:* Queen's Lower School pupils showing off the new link between Sandford House and Nedham House , November 2004.

Arts, crafts and Toys!

Some shop windows of our childhood are never forgotten. Going shopping with mother often involved repeatedly tugging on her arm and demanding 'can we go home now?'

But there were also those shops where the reverse would occur: shop windows to which we pressed our little noses, and from which we, not mother, had always to be dragged unwillingly away.

Happily there are also shops which exert equal fascination on both youngsters and their parents.

Top: Gladys Hutcheson with one of her exquisite costume dolls. Right: Donald Hutcheson, son of Beatrice who opened the toy shop shortly after the Second World War. Below: The Arts & Crafts toy department, 1953.

Chester's Arts & Crafts Studio celebrated its 80th anniversary in 2004 by moving round the corner, from St Michael's Row to new premises in Bridge Street Row.

The new shop was extensively refurbished and fitted out to a high standard with air conditioning, a lift for customers and wooden floors.

Brothers Nick and Mike Hutcheson who, together with their wives, run the shop today, are the third generation of the family in the business which they took over from their late father Donald.

The shop, on two floors, is much more spacious than its predecessor. At Row level there is a fine collection of needlework, knitting wool, crafts and collectibles. The toy, model and hobby department, situated on the first floor, is an irresistible magnet for young and old alike, specialising in model

railways, scalextric, games, die cast models, radio control, lego and construction kits

When Beatrice Hutcheson's daughter, Gladys, was stricken with polio Beatrice started the first Arts and Crafts Studio. It opened in 1924 in the Old Central Buildings in Pepper Street. There Gladys worked and trained other girls in the crafts of leather work and needlework. By the late 1920s there was such a demand for the suede belts which Gladys made out of leaf motif that she could hardly keep up the supply.

There was a move in 1928 to Northgate Street. Rooms were taken over what was later Halfords. There ten girls were employed in tooling leather, making fashion accessories. As well as a workshop there was a room for display and sales, but as it had no window on to the street to catch the attention of passers-by Beatrice decided on another move.

In 1933 Beatrice took a lease on a shop premises in St Michael's Arcade. Trade here was difficult as the arcade was a cul-de-sac, but Beatrice managed to make a name for herself before most of the workroom girls were taken away for the war effort. In addition to its belts the firm made trimmings, beautiful leather goods, beaten brassware, hand-painted mirrors and fashion accessories.

In the post-war years the shop bought in more varied goods for sale, including fine lace, tableware, baskets and Hummel porcelain from Germany - for which the shop is still a major outlet. Gladys meanwhile continued with her

needlework, making exquisite dolls in international costumes for which the shop was renowned for 30 years. Working six days a week from her work room at home Gladys turned out dozens a day.

Shortly after the war, Beatrice's son Donald had taken what had until then been the Red Cross premises opposite the craft shop; he opened a toy shop featuring such unforgettable names as Dinky, Meccano and Hornby. In 1976 this took over the shop next door to expand further. The basement model department was a Mecca for the collectors of model railways, diecast models, kits and the radio-control enthusiast.

An independent family business for over 80 years, but still moving with the times, the toy shop department now has the support of 'Youngsters' toy buying group (which has a turnover in excess of £100,000,000). That support gives buying power that ensures low prices. Through careful selection from tens of thousands of toys available, the shop can offer some 5,000 lines, all chosen for quality, safety and play value. It can also offer collectors' models that may well become the valuable heirlooms of the future.

The art and craft department continues to be a major supplier of all forms of needlework, from counted cross stitch to tapestry, alongside all the ancillary threads, canvas, ribbons and trimmings as well as still being a major outlet for the world-famous Hummel porcelain figures.

For more than eight decades Chester's Arts & Crafts Studio has been a focus of fascination for local folk and their

families both young and old. Today that fascination shows no signs of waning - and there are still noses being pressed against its windows.

*Top: Manageress Carol Evans in the new toy department, 2005. **Above left:** Nick Hutcheson in the model department, 1997. **Left:** The Arts & Crafts Studio new Bridge Street premises, 2005.*

To market to market

There's something about a market that makes it a far more memorable experience than going shopping elsewhere. The sense of smell is the one most deeply embedded in the human brain and it can take no more than the scent of a fresh orange to take us back in our mind's eye to childhood and hear again the shout of a greengrocer calling out his wares.

Markets are universal phenomenon. Every town in the world has a market. In early Britain, and in third world countries today, nothing fancy was needed, not even a stall. A pitch can be something as simple as a blanket on the ground - sometimes not even that.

The attraction for market traders is the low cost involved. Conversely, for those wishing to buy, there is the attraction that those low overheads can be passed on to the consumer. There's always a bargain to be found at a market.

The city of Chester has been benefiting from the existence of a market since early Roman times. The earliest traders no doubt found Chester particularly attractive because of the presence of large numbers of soldiers with money to spend.

No trace now remains of those first market traders, but we can find solid evidence that the lively city of Chester has been attracting discerning shoppers, and those with an eye

Above: The market exterior pictured in the 1960s.
Below and right: Early market stalls.

for a bargain, for nearly a thousand years.

The earliest written mention of the existence of a market in Chester was in the year 1139, it was not until some decades later however that a market charter was first officially granted. The city's first shopping charter was, in fact, officially issued in the year 1208. The document stated that, 'the men of Chester and their heirs' were to be granted the privilege of sole selling rights. Those rights extended to everything except to the annual fairs which were, by contrast, to be open to all traders. In 1239 those rights were confirmed by Henry III. The privilege of sole selling rights being vested in the men of Chester continued unchanged until 1506, the year in which the Great Charter was passed, and which also granted Chester its first Mayor.

No doubt 'the men of Chester and their heirs' were not particularly pleased at the loss of their trading monopoly. The people of Chester would however benefit by the expansion of the market and from the price competition which came when outsiders were at last permitted to trade.

With their sharp eye for business, new and old traders of Chester not only took advantage of the opportunities they were granted but expanded those opportunities to include, amongst many other enterprises, coal and cattle markets. Chester's rows and rows of traders built up a fine reputation that spread far and wide: the now famous Rows were originally named after those lines of traders.

As their individual names suggest the Rows themselves were specialised and consisted of many different types of traders. Amongst them was a Shoemakers Row, a Cooks Row and an Ironmongers Row. There was also a Pepper Alley and a Fish Shambles. To those Rows would subsequently be added the Linen Hall and the Fruit, Root and Herb Market.

Horse, cloth and cheese fairs were also held in the city. Those fairs

were the forerunners of the magnificent array of shops that can be found in the city today, but it is to the market that we are paying particular attention.

The Chester market used to be situated on Northgate Street next to the Town Hall. The Market Hall in Northgate Street, which traded for over a century, was opened on the 10th of March, 1863. Memorably that day was also the Prince of Wales' wedding day! The market traded successfully from this location for more than 100 years, until 1967, when it was relocated to its current site in Princess Street.

Today, run by Chester City Council, the market in Princess Street opens six days a week, from Monday to Saturday. Within it are up to 100 stalls offering a wide choice of the finest quality produce, from foodstuffs to flowers, cosmetics and millinery.

Nearly two thousand years after the first market stalls appeared in Chester business still shows no sign of slacking.

This page: *The familiar sight of a busy market in the 1960s.*

Still wearing well

Tradition takes many guises. For some it is found in our architectural heritage. For others it is encapsulated in the way we celebrate our history. But more than this our traditional way is something which we observe daily: the way we speak, our polite behaviour and above all, visible to everyone, the way we dress.

The story of Cochranes, the traditional menswear specialists, located today in Bridge Street Row, has a history dating to 1903 when William Cochrane opened his first Gentleman's Outfitters at Chester Cross.

William and his wife had previously owned shops in Liverpool, Southport and Preston. As a step towards semi-retirement the couple sold those shops and moved to Chester where they traded as The Belfast Shirt and Collar Company before

Above: Founder William Cochrane.
Top: An early interior of Cochranes.
Right: Cochranes 37 Bridge Street Row premises.

renaming the business as Ye Olde Tan Glove Shoppe. The shop, specialising in socks, gloves and regimental ties proved to be extremely popular, boasting amongst its distinguished customers the Duchess of Westminster who frequently bought ladies' gloves from the Cochrane's.

Increasing sales enabled Mrs Cochrane to open another shop, Camilla at 39 Bridge Street Row, this time specialising in ladieswear. Mrs Cochrane however started to introduce menswear to the shop, and phase out ladies' clothing.

Around 1920, the business moved to 37 Bridge Street Row under the new name of WM Cochrane, trading in ladieswear and as a milliners. The new the shop was to have only a brief period as a ladieswear specialist: when Mrs Cochrane retired in 1926, her husband switched the focus to menswear.

The Cochranes had four sons, two of whom worked in the family business. William was eventually put in charge of the Cross shop and Bruce in charge of the shop at 37 Bridge Street Row. In 1935 the business became a Limited company and during the following decade, despite the outbreak of war in 1939, would experience little disruption, the only one being the absence of one of its employees, Mr Just, who was called up for service in the armed forces, but who returned in 1944. Mr Just subsequently became Managing Director, a role which he would fill until the mid 1980s.

In the post war years Cochranes reputation in Chester continued to grow. The shop stocked several well known brands at the time including, Double Two and Viyella. The shirts were all cotton, had detachable collars, and had to be in white, blue or cream! The prices of the stock also differed in comparison with today's prices. In 1953 a raincoat cost, £7.10.0, whilst now it would cost over £200. In 1949 a suit cost £8 15s 8d compared to about £300 in the shop today

How many readers still recall the once-familiar brown shop front, with its green tiles, in the Victorian Arcade. In 1964 however the shop underwent a refit, the old glass and mahogany counters were replaced with modern fixtures and the lighting was improved.

Despite such modernisation it was not until 1970 that the time-honoured procedure of writing receipts on dockets was replaced with the use of a modern cash register

The 1980s too saw many changes. Leisure wear started to become popular with the arrival of more foreign

holidays: the shop's stock became gradually more and more colourful as did the window displays, which now became a sales feature.

With the help of its Managing Director, Mr Hancock, Cochranes changed with the times, though without abandoning its traditions or alienating its long-standing customers.

Due to large increases in rent and rates, the shop at Chester Cross had to be closed in 1987. The company now concentrated its efforts on the success of the shop in Bridge Street Row. The following year Mr Hancock retired to be followed by Mr Seed who now became Managing Director of Cochrane's and continued to maintain the company's success.

In 1990, the shop front was painted green and gold. In 1999, the shop underwent further changes being refurbished with a up-to-date but still traditional look.

Michael Hall became Managing Director in 1998, under him progress has continued: fixtures, fittings, decor and lighting on both floors have all been replaced and modernised. But whatever refurbishments and other innovations there may have been Cochranes still remains determined to preserve its hard-won and well-deserved reputation for tradition and expertise.

Top left: *An early window display.*
Above: *Michael Hall, Managing Director.*
Below: *Cochranes in the late 1980s.*

The best days of our lives

The King's School in Chester was founded in 1541 during the reign of King Henry VIII, following the dissolution of the religious houses. The statutes provided that there should be twenty-four 'poor and friendless' boys between the ages of nine and fifteen, who were to receive £3 6s 8d a year each to be taught to speak and write Latin. There was to be a headmaster (with a salary of £22 per year) and an usher or second master (salary £10). The school was variously called 'The Free School' or 'The Grammar School'. It was not known as The King's School until the mid 19th century when it was referred to as the 'Grammar School of King Henry VIII'.

From the earliest times, the 24 foundationers were augmented by private pupils who boarded in the Headmaster's House. One of the earliest of these is thought to be Sir Thomas Francisse, physician to Queen Elizabeth I. By 1783, both the Headmaster, Rev. Thomas Bancroft and his assistant master had boarders. An advertisement states '... his intention of taking to Board, four young Gentlemen at twenty-five guineas yearly, washing excluded.' One of these pupils was George Ormerod who later became a well known Cheshire historian.

For most of its early years, the school was housed in the old monastic refectory, though records show the school located elsewhere within the Abbey Court for several years due to the poor condition of the refectory. Very little is known of the school during the Civil War, but we do know that the Headmaster John Greenhalgh was ejected for showing favour to the Royalists. The historian, Thomas Hughes, himself an old boy, referred to the scholars of the day as the 'Roundhead scholars'.

In 1869 the Schools Inquiry Commission reported that there were 70 boys in the school (only two of whom were boarders), with a headmaster and two assistants. Latin, Greek, French and drawing were taught. The school had no classrooms or playground and was badly overcrowded. Four years later, the school was reorganised under the Endowed Schools Act, 1869 and separated from the cathedral foundation. New buildings were erected at a cost of £16,000 and formally opened by William Gladstone in 1876. They adjoined the cathedral on the north west and provided accommodation for up to 200 boys. Chemistry and art were now added to the curriculum. That same year 'By the kindness of the Duke of Westminster the school has the use of a large playing field in the suburbs'. The six acres about a mile from the school provided excellent facilities for many years.

Throughout the late 19th century and into the early 20th century, the school ran a Boarding House under the charge

Top: The Grammar School from Cloister Court of Chester Cathedral in the early nineteenth century.
Left: Masters at The King's School 1885.
Below: Rowing crew with their coach, Rev. G.A. Vesey, in 1902.

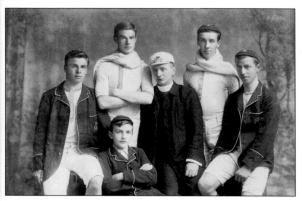

some of the playing fields were ploughed up and used to produce crops. Pupils helped on local farms, collected scrap metal, trained as First Aid workers and contributed in many other ways towards the war effort.

As pupil numbers rose during the 1940s, part of the former Bluecoat School buildings in Upper Northgate Street was taken over on a 10 year lease. However, an inspection report in 1949 stated that accommodation was out of date and inadequate for the growing school.

The school had already recognised its shortcomings and had signed a 999 year lease with the Eaton Estate for a 32 acre site on the Wrexham Road. Designing new school buildings started in 1956, and in 1960 the whole school moved to the new site. More buildings followed in 1964 and 1971. In the first decade on the new site the school grew by almost 10% to reach 535 boys.

Plant-a-tree year in 1973 resulted in 170 new trees planted with the assistance of the Chief Forester of the Duke of Westminster. 1975 saw The Cathedral Choir School incorporated into King's. In 1989, HRH Princess Margaret formally opened more new buildings including a sixth form centre and sports hall. Expansion continued into the 1990s. Girls joined the sixth form for the first time in 1998 and in 2003 the school became fully co-educational - though the first recorded girl had in fact arrived as far back as 1974! At the same time the school embarked on another major development programme.

In 2005, the flourishing school has more than 800 students in the combined Senior and Junior Schools. Former pupils can look back on their school days with pride knowing that they are part of Chester's great history.

Top left: The Cadet Corps outside the school in 1916.
Above left: Her Majesty Queen Elizabeth the Queen Mother at the official opening of the new school buildings in June 1960. *Below:* The King's School from the Wrexham Road, 1999.

of one of the masters. In 1885, this was located at 98, Watergate Flags, but later moved to Eaton Road. By 1911, the governors had acquired premises formerly used by Arnold House, a private school in Walpole Street. This became the new school boarding house and also the Junior School.

During the Great War, games were replaced by military training. A Cadet Corps was founded in 1916 which all boys were expected to join. Shooting practice took place every day of the week. Rough grass land at Arnold House was dug and planted with potatoes. Senior boys helped with the hay harvests in the summer and others assisted in the national re-afforestation programme.

The interwar years saw the arrival of typewriters, the installation of electricity in 1922 and a telephone exchange. A tuck shop was built and manned by the school prefects. The school purchased its own playing fields on the site of the Royal Agricultural Show ground facing Lache Lane. In 1931, the boarding house part of Arnold House was closed due to lack of boys wishing to board.

Major changes became necessary during the Second World War. Parts of the cathedral were adapted as air raid shelters,

A *fitting farewell*

O nly two things are certain in life: taxes and death. We may avoid the former but none of us can avoid the latter. But if we cannot avoid saying farewell to our loved ones we can at least see that the final farewell is a fitting one. And the best way to ensure that such arrangements are handled with all due dignity and decorum is to employ an experienced funeral director.

Dutton and Hallmark is one of the few remaining independent, family run funeral directors in the Chester area. The company has a history which tells the tale of two fiercely competing firms which finally resolved their differences to become united in both business and friendship.

Exactly when the Dutton family entered the funeral directing business is unknown. One Thomas Dutton however, was working as a coffin maker as long ago as 1704. His great grandson, Edgar Dutton, founded the firm of Edgar Dutton and Sons in the 1850s.

At the start of the 19th century Caleb Dutton, Edgar's father, owned a funeral directors business in Forgate Street Chester. In his youth Edgar had worked for his father in the business. That experience proved to be invaluable when later in life

Edgar set up his own firm. Edgar established his new business at Lower Bridge Street where he began trading as a Funeral Directors and Carriage Proprietor.

With the help of his sons, John James and George Henry, Edgar's business soon began to flourish, quickly gaining a fine

Top: *Founder Edgar Dutton with his back to the camera, Harry holding the horse and John James in the doorway.*
Above: *William Henry Hallmark outside Overleigh Cemetery, 1920s.*

the first world war, when the firm had to organise many servicemen's funerals despite the absence of many young members of staff away serving their country in war. That was not the end of horses however: in the 1930s, when Edgar's grandsons, Edgar junior and Thomas, took over the running of the still thriving business, Edgar Dutton and Sons had became the last local funeral directors to still offer horse-drawn funerals.

By contrast with Duttons WH Hallmark and Sons experienced difficulties during these years and went into receivership, twice. The business was bought by the Griffin family in the 1940s who ran it successfully until 1974.

reputation with both the people of Chester and beyond.

Edgar Dutton and his sons' trade, as makers of coffins and suppliers of hearses and carriages, also won it a high reputation with other funeral directors and amongst the wheelwrights with whom they conducted business.

Edgar became successful enough to be able to move his business to new and better premises at 9 Frodsham Street. It was there that Edgar Dutton first met and became friendly with the Hallmark family. The Hallmarks owned a catering business, W H Hallmark and Sons. Soon Edgar began passing business their way, Edgar using their services to cater for funeral parties.

In 1860, Edgar Dutton and Sons were able to move again, this time to 30 Frodsham Street, where they stayed for over a century.

Together the two businesses, Duttons and Hallmarks, thrived. Unhappily, in 1890 the Hallmarks decided to set up in business as a funeral directors on their own. As a consequence, the two families became sworn enemies and did not speak to one another for the next 30 years - not even to congratulate Edgar Dutton when in 1902 he was made the Sheriff of Chester.

In 1910 Duttons began to provide motorised funerals. Using motor vehicles rather than horses became important during

WH Hallmark and Sons, and Edgar Dutton and Sons both closed their businesses in 1974: both due to ill health and problems with premises.

Happily that was not the end of the story. Edgar's great grandson, Stephen Dutton decided to follow his great grand-father and set up a funeral directors business under the name, Dutton and Hallmark.

The business soon returned to the former success. In 1997, with tradition in mind, horse-drawn funerals were reintro-duced - though for those who still prefer a limousine the business also operates the largest Rolls-Royce funeral fleet in the area.

Today, Stephen Dutton takes great pride in his family's history and aims to follow tradition, providing the bereaved of Chester with a truly personal farewell service.

Top left: *Edgar Dutton conducting a funeral, circa 1912.*
Above left: *Edgar Dutton & Son's team during the second world war.* ***Below:*** *The company's new Armstrong-Siddeley fleet in 1958.*

A home from home

Crabwall Hall Residential Home in Mollington opened in 1989. The purpose-built home incorporates an attractive former dairy farm dating back centuries.

Richard Cadwaladr, the son of one of Cheshire's best known farming families, moved from Two Mile House, the family home, to Crabwall Hall Farm in 1970 together with his wife Sue and their one year old daughter Sally Ann.

At first Richard still continued to work within the family business, and together they ran four farms, with dairy farming just one aspect of the work. However, in 1983 due to Richard's failing health he and Sue made the decision to leave the family business and run Crabwall Hall Farm alone. Despite Richard's poor health he and Sue continued to play a large part in Cheshire society, with numerous events held at Crabwall in support of local charities such as Muscular Dystrophy and the RSPCA.

Several factors contributed to their eventual diversification into the caring industry, not least Richard's ill-health and the serious decline in the UK's farming industry. Yet the final decision came when Sue's great aunt was placed in a home in North Wales: she was desperately unhappy, so the Cadwaladrs vowed that they would set up a residential home of their own, one where people could live a fulfilling existence surrounded by loving carers in a pleasant happy atmosphere.

Their ambition was achieved in 1989 when Crabwall Hall officially opened its doors to the public, with a staff of 11 and beds for 12 residents. Since then it has grown and now has a staff of 39 and is home for 32 elderly

Top left: Richard and Sue Cadwaladr, founders of Crabwall Hall Residential Home. **Above right:** *Sue Cadwaladr and The Duke of Westminster at the official opening ceremony of Crabwall Hall.* **Right:** *Sue Cadwaladr and staff welcome their first residents, 1989.*

residents. Each of the 32 rooms features en-suite facilities, telephone and television. There is a large lounge and dining area in addition to a library and conservatory. Daily activities include visiting entertainers, shopping trips, quizzes and exercise classes.

Over the years there have been many occasions of celebration such as the official opening conducted by the Duke of Westminster in 1992, and the honour of winning the annual Chester in Bloom Gardening Prize for the glorious gardens surrounding Crabwall Hall. A most memorable event was the 103rd birthday party of Miss Kitty Spendlove which was attended not only by friends and family but also by the Lord Mayor and Lady Mayoress of Chester.

Tragically Richard and Sue's eldest daughter Sally Ann passed away suddenly of an asthma attack in December 1998 after being married for just 18 months to Captain Jason Jordan of the Cheshire Regiment.

Richard had earlier suffered from a number of severe strokes, leaving him unable to comprehend the loss; he would require 24 hour care until his death in 2001.

Throughout these times Sue and Sophia would have been unable to carry on without the love, care and support of the staff and residents who displayed the essence of all that Crabwall has come to mean, a true family.

It is a tribute to Richard and Sue that the business they built up together was, by its very nature, able to support the family through those difficult times.

Since Richard's passing the Cadwaladrs' youngest daughter Sophia, a Management Graduate from the University of Sheffield, has joined the family business; together Sue and Sophia are the proprietors of Crabwall Hall.

Crabwall Hall continues very much as a small family-run business with Sue's brothers now also part of the team: Tony Muff is the head chef after running 'The Floral', an extremely successful restaurant in Llandudno. Sue's eldest brother, Derek Muff, has become the Maintenance Manager after retiring as a master carpenter. And the family link does not stop there! 'Muff's the Butchers' of Bromborough, a company established by Jack Muff, Sue's father, and now run by her youngest brother Stephen, provide their award-winning sausages to the Home.

Set in acres of rolling countryside with views overlooking the Welsh hills and with its delightful gardens, today Crabwall Hall Care Home continues to provide a tranquil haven where residents can live with dignity supported by a fully trained team of exceptional and caring staff.

*Top left: Sophia Cadwaladr pictured with Mrs Kitty Spendlove on her 103rd birthday, also pictured is Mrs Spendlove's niece. **Above right:** Crabwall Hall Residential Home. **Left:** The Cadwaladr family; Richard and Susan with daughters Sally Ann (right) and Sophia.*

Enriching the future at Capenhurst

If history began with the Stone Age, followed by the Bronze Age and the Iron Age then what might future historians call our own times? Some suggest the Nuclear Age.

The age of the Atom arrived in 1945, brought about by the imperatives of war. But the enormous energy released by nuclear fission could be applied to peace as well as war. By the 1950s the dream of almost limitless electrical power created using controlled atomic reactions was being turned into practical reality in Britain and the USA. In power stations, ships and submarines bulky coal and oil were to be replaced by more efficient nuclear fuels for the first time.

Located near Chester, Urenco's Capenhurst site is part of Urenco Limited, a European energy company which supplies the international nuclear industry with uranium enrichment services and advanced enrichment technologies and expertise. The site operates three plants producing enriched uranium for civil use to enable nuclear power stations to generate clean carbon emission free electricity. Urenco's production plants at Capenhurst and in Europe all employ state-of-the-art enrichment technology based on the gas centrifuge process, the cleanest and most energy-efficient system.

The group operates in the global uranium enrichment market, part of the nuclear fuel cycle. This leads to the generation of clean, carbon emission free electricity. Urenco is committed to supporting sustainable energy generation and nuclear energy is increasingly viewed as the obvious commercial choice to provide a sustainable energy supply.

The Capenhurst site employs over 300 people and provides the local community with long-term jobs in a technical environment, as well as opportunities for young people to pursue engineering and scientific careers. Urenco is an independent, international energy and technology group operating from plants in Germany, the Netherlands and the United Kingdom. Its focus is on providing safe, cost effective and reliable uranium enrichment services for civil power generation.

Urenco Limited is a UK-registered company based in Marlow, Buckinghamshire. Marketing in North America is carried out by Urenco Inc., located in Washington DC.

Urenco (Capenhurst) Limited became a wholly owned subsidiary of Urenco in 1993 following a restructuring of the Group. Since then the site has expanded its production capacity almost threefold.

The success of Urenco has been built on the technological edge of its centrifuge enrichment process. This

major competitive advantage results from both the technical expertise of its employees and their dedication and commitment.

Urenco also has considerable experience in operating enrichment plants. These plants generate reliable low cost uranium enrichment that provides customers with secured supplies at predictable prices.

In addition to Urenco's contribution to the local economy, the Capenhurst site takes a role as an active and responsible member of the community.

Capenhurst has a long record of involvement with the communities around the site and is continually seeking ways to communicate with local people and enhance the benefits they gain from the site's presence.

Employees are also major supporters of the Capenhurst site's Medical and Research Fund, a monthly lottery competition which has distributed more than £300,000 to good causes.

Through financial contributions, and the voluntary efforts of many of its employees, the company supports a wide range of projects and initiatives covering cultural activities, education, sport and charitable organisations. Urenco interacts with local schools to encourage and nurture an interest in science and engineering through the provision of workshops and student award programmes. Sponsorship is also provided for the arts such as the Royal Liverpool Philharmonic Orchestra and the Wirral Junior Orchestra.

The company liaises closely with local schools and charities in order to gain an understanding of community needs and works in partnership with a number of agencies to add value to local initiatives. Sponsorship covers a wide range of activities ranging from providing schools with special dictionaries, to bulbs for planting and theatre trips for specific school groups. The company has also contributed to the funding of a top class running track for a local athletics club.

Urenco is also a long-term provider of summer placements for undergraduates and is extensively involved in providing work experience for pupils and organising industry and business awareness initiatives with local schools.

School children whose history lessons cover the Stone Age and the Steam Age can be proud to know that today they live in the age of nuclear energy.

Pictures: Views of the Urenco Capenhurst site.

Acknowledgments

The publishers would like to thank

Chester Library, Libraries & Archives, Chester County Council

Andrew Mitchell

Steve Ainsworth

True North Books Ltd - Book List

Memories of Accrington - 1 903204 05 4

Memories of Barnet - 1 903204 16 X

Memories of Barnsley - 1 900463 11 3

More Memories of Barnsley - 1 903 204 79 8

Golden Years of Barnsley -1 900463 87 3

Memories of Basingstoke - 1 903204 26 7

Memories of Bedford - 1 900463 83 0

More Memories of Bedford - 1 903204 33 X

Golden Years of Birmingham - 1 900463 04 0

Birmingham Memories - 1 903204 45 3

More Birmingham Memories - 1 903204 80 1

Memories of Blackburn - 1 900463 40 7

More Memories of Blackburn - 1 900463 96 2

Memories of Blackpool - 1 900463 21 0

Memories of Bolton - 1 900463 45 8

More Memories of Bolton - 1 900463 13 X

Bolton Memories - 1 903204 37 2

Memories of Bournemouth -1 900463 44 X

Memories of Bradford - 1 900463 00 8

More Memories of Bradford - 1 900463 16 4

More Memories of Bradford II - 1 900463 63 6

Bradford Memories - 1 903204 47 X

Bradford City Memories - 1 900463 57 1

Memories of Bristol - 1 900463 78 4

More Memories of Bristol - 1 903204 43 7

Memories of Bromley - 1 903204 21 6

Memories of Burnley - 1 900463 95 4

Golden Years of Burnley - 1 900463 67 9

Memories of Bury - 1 900463 90 3

More Memories of Bury - 1 903 204 78 X

Memories of Cambridge - 1 900463 88 1

Memories of Cardiff - 1 900463 14 8

More Memories of Cardiff - 1 903204 73 9

Memories of Carlisle - 1 900463 38 5

Memories of Chelmsford - 1 903204 29 1

Memories of Cheltenham - 1 903204 17 8

Memories of Chester - 1 900463 46 6

More Memories of Chester -1 903204 02 X

Memories of Chesterfield -1 900463 61 X

More Memories of Chesterfield - 1 903204 28 3

Memories of Colchester - 1 900463 74 1

Nostalgic Coventry - 1 900463 58 X

Coventry Memories - 1 903204 38 0

Memories of Croydon - 1 900463 19 9

More Memories of Croydon - 1 903204 35 6

Golden Years of Darlington - 1 900463 72 5

Nostalgic Darlington - 1 900463 31 8

Darlington Memories - 1 903204 46 1

Memories of Derby - 1 900463 37 7

More Memories of Derby - 1 903204 20 8

Memories of Dewsbury & Batley - 1 900463 80 6

Memories of Doncaster - 1 900463 36 9

More Memories of Doncaster - 1 903204 75 5

Nostalgic Dudley - 1 900463 03 2

Golden Years of Dudley - 1 903204 60 7

Memories of Edinburgh - 1 900463 33 4

More memories of Edinburgh - 1903204 72 0

Memories of Enfield - 1 903204 14 3

Memories of Exeter - 1 900463 94 6

Memories of Glasgow - 1 900463 68 7

More Memories of Glasgow - 1 903204 44 5

Memories of Gloucester - 1 903204 04 6

Memories of Grimsby - 1 900463 97 0

More Memories of Grimsby - 1 903204 36 4

Memories of Guildford - 1 903204 22 4

Memories of Halifax - 1 900463 05 9

More Memories of Halifax - 1 900463 06 7

Golden Years of Halifax - 1 900463 62 8

Nostalgic Halifax - 1 903204 30 5

Memories of Harrogate - 1 903204 01 1

Memories of Hartlepool - 1 900463 42 3

Memories of High Wycombe - 1 900463 84 9

Memories of Huddersfield - 1 900463 15 6

More Memories of Huddersfield - 1 900463 26 1

Golden Years of Huddersfield - 1 900463 77 6

Nostalgic Huddersfield - 1 903204 19 4

Huddersfield Town FC - 1 900463 51 2

Memories of Hull - 1 900463 86 5

More Memories of Hull - 1 903204 06 2

Hull Memories - 1 903204 70 4

Memories of Ipswich - 1 900463 09 1

More Memories of Ipswich - 1 903204 52 6

True North Books Ltd - Book List

Memories of Kingston - 1 903204 24 0

Memories of Leeds - 1 900463 75 X

More Memories of Leeds - 1 900463 12 1

Golden Years of Leeds - 1 903204 07 0

Memories of Leicester - 1 900463 08 3

Leeds Memories - 1 903204 62 3

More Memories of Leicester - 1 903204 08 9

Memories of Leigh - 1 903204 27 5

Memories of Lincoln - 1 900463 43 1

Memories of Liverpool - 1 900463 07 5

More Memories of Liverpool - 1 903204 09 7

Liverpool Memories - 1 903204 53 4

Memories of Luton - 1 900463 93 8

Memories of Macclesfield - 1 900463 28 8

Memories of Manchester - 1 900463 27 X

More Memories of Manchester - 1 903204 03 8

Manchester Memories - 1 903204 54 2

Memories of Middlesbrough - 1 900463 56 3

More Memories of Middlesbrough - 1 903204 42 9

Memories of Newbury - 1 900463 79 2

Memories of Newcastle - 1 900463 81 4

More Memories of Newcastle - 1 903204 10 0

Newcastle Memories - 1.903204 71 2

Memories of Newport - 1 900463 59 8

Memories of Northampton - 1 900463 48 2

More Memories of Northampton - 1 903204 34 8

Memories of Norwich - 1 900463 73 3

Memories of Nottingham - 1 900463 91 1

More Memories of Nottingham - 1 903204 11 9

Nottingham Memories - 1 903204 63 1

Bygone Oldham - 1 900463 25 3

Memories of Oldham - 1 900463 76 8

Memories of Oxford - 1 900463 54 7

Memories of Peterborough - 1 900463 98 9

Golden Years of Poole - 1 900463 69 5

Memories of Portsmouth - 1 900463 39 3

More Memories of Portsmouth - 1 903204 51 8

Nostalgic Preston - 1 900463 50 4

More Memories of Preston - 1 900463 17 2

Preston Memories - 1 903204 41 0

Memories of Reading - 1 900463 49 0

Memories of Rochdale - 1 900463 60 1

More Memories of Reading - 1 903204 39 9

More Memories of Rochdale - 1 900463 22 9

Memories of Romford - 1 903204 40 2

Memories of Rothertham- 1903204 77 1

Memories of St Albans - 1 903204 23 2

Memories of St Helens - 1 900463 52 0

Memories of Sheffield - 1 900463 20 2

More Memories of Sheffield - 1 900463 32 6

Golden Years of Sheffield - 1 903204 13 5

Memories of Slough - 1 900 463 29 6

Golden Years of Solihull - 1 903204 55 0

Memories of Southampton - 1 900463 34 2

More Memories of Southampton - 1 903204 49 6

Memories of Stockport - 1 900463 55 5

More Memories of Stockport - 1 903204 18 6

Memories of Stockton - 1 900463 41 5

Memories of Stoke-on-Trent - 1 900463 47 4

More Memories of Stoke-on-Trent - 1 903204 12 7

Memories of Stourbridge - 1903204 31 3

Memories of Sunderland - 1 900463 71 7

More Memories of Sunderland - 1 903204 48 8

Memories of Swindon - 1 903204 00 3

Memories of Uxbridge - 1 900463 64 4

Memories of Wakefield - 1 900463 65 2

More Memories of Wakefield - 1 900463 89 X

Nostalgic Walsall - 1 900463 18 0

Golden Years of Walsall - 1 903204 56 9

More Memories of Warrington - 1 900463 02 4

Memories of Watford - 1 900463 24 5

Golden Years of West Bromwich - 1 900463 99 7

Memories of Wigan - 1 900463 85 7

Golden Years of Wigan - 1 900463 82 2

More Memories of Wigan - 1 903204 82 8

Nostalgic Wirral - 1 903204 15 1

Wirral Memories - 1 903204 747

Memories of Woking - 1 903204 32 1

Nostalgic Wolverhampton - 1 900463 53 9

Wolverhampton Memories - 1 903204 50 X

Memories of Worcester - 1 903204 25 9

Memories of Wrexham - 1 900463 23 7

Memories of York - 1 900463 66 0